D1635827

THE
FINALISTS

**EXCERPTS FROM THE FIVE 2006
COSTA AWARD-WINNING BOOKS**

Published by Costa Publishing

The Finalists:
Excerpts from the five 2006 Costa Award-winning books

First published in Great Britain in 2006 by
Costa Publishing
Whitbread PLC
Whitbread Court
Houghton Hall Business Park
Porz Avenue
Dunstable
Bedfordshire LU5 5XE

A CIP catalogue record for this book is available
from the British Library.

ISBN 978-0-9554863-0-2

Designed and typeset in Trade Gothic and Adobe Garamond by Meteorite.
Printed in Great Britain by Lamport Gilbert Limited, 3 Darwin Close,
Reading, Berkshire RG2 0TB.

INTRODUCTION

We're in great company at Costa in our 35th year, sharing our landmark birthday with one of the UK's most prestigious and popular book prizes.

Since 1971 the Whitbread Book Awards – now the Costa Book Awards – have honoured some of the best books of the year by writers based in the UK or Ireland. We're delighted to be sponsoring the awards for the first time in 2006, building on such an important literary heritage.

From 580 books, our dedicated judging panels chose five category winners – a novel, a first novel, a biography, a children's book and a collection of poetry.

We'd like to give you an exclusive, bite-sized preview of these winning books, now shortlisted for the overall Costa Book of the Year – and five fantastic reasons to linger a little longer at your local Costa.

A double life, a brutal crime, a warm and wistful memoir, a love letter to Nigeria and a house of shocking secrets…

Lose yourself in these stunning pieces of writing and meet the fascinating, frightening and fabulous characters that inhabit this collection of the finest books of 2006.

There's nothing quite like relaxing with a good book and a cup of coffee. I'd like to invite you to sit back with your favourite cup of Costa and savour The Finalists.

John Derkach

Managing Director, Costa

Visit the website at **www.costabookawards.com**

THE COSTA FOUNDATION

We are committed to supporting the communities from which we source our coffee beans.

All profits from sales of *The Finalists* will go to the Costa Foundation, set up to help improve the social and economic welfare of our suppliers in developing countries. The Foundation is investing in water sanitation, nutrition and education programmes in countries including Colombia, Ethiopia, Uganda and Kenya.

Thanks for helping us help our coffee-growing communities.

CONTENTS

The Tenderness of Wolves by Stef Penney
Copyright © 2006 by Stef Penney
First published in Great Britain in 2006 by Quercus,
21 Bloomsbury Square, London WC1A 2NS
www.quercusbooks.co.uk

Restless by William Boyd
Copyright © 2006 by William Boyd
First published in Great Britain in 2006 by Bloomsbury Publishing Plc,
36 Soho Square, London W1D 3QY
www.bloomsbury.com

Keeping Mum by Brian Thompson
Copyright © 2006 by Brian Thompson
First published in Great Britain in 2006 by Atlantic Books,
an imprint of Grove Atlantic Ltd, Ormond House,
26-27 Boswell Street,London WC1N 3JZ
www.groveatlantic.co.uk

Letter to Patience by John Haynes
Copyright © 2006 by John Haynes
First published in Great Britain in 2006 by Seren, an imprint of
Poetry Wales Press Ltd, 57 Nolton Street, Bridgend, Wales, CF31 3AE
www.seren-books.com
The publisher acknowledges the financial assistance of the Welsh Books Council.

Set in Stone by Linda Newbery
Copyright © 2006 by Linda Newbery
First published in Great Britain in 2006 by David Fickling Books,
31 Beaumont Street, Oxford OX1 2NP, a division of Random House
Children's Books, 61-63 Uxbridge Road, London W5 5SA,
a division of the Random House Group Limited Reg No 954009
www.kidsatrandomhouse.co.uk

THE TENDERNESS OF WOLVES

by **Stef Penney**

Quercus

THE TENDERNESS OF WOLVES

by **Stef Penney**

1867, Canada. As winter tightens its grip on the isolated settlement of Dove River, a man is brutally murdered and a seventeen-year-old boy disappears. Tracks leaving the dead man's cabin head north towards the forest and the tundra beyond. In the wake of such violence, people are drawn to the township – journalists, Hudson's Bay Company men, trappers, traders – but do they want to solve the crime, or exploit it?

Stef Penney grew up in Edinburgh. After a degree in Philosophy and Theology from Bristol University and a variety of jobs in this country and abroad, she turned to film-making. She studied Film and TV at Bournemouth College of Art and on graduation was selected for the Carlton Television New Writers Scheme. Stef lives in East London.

"The Tenderness of Wolves stood out from a very strong shortlist. We felt enveloped by the snowy landscape and gripped by the beautiful writing and effortless story-telling. It is a story of love, suspense and beauty. We couldn't put it down."

Judges
Alyson Rudd – Writer, The Times
Sophie Kinsella – Author
Andrew McClellan – Fiction Buyer, WH Smith

For my parents

DISAPPEARANCE

THE LAST TIME I saw Laurent Jammet, he was in Scott's store with a dead wolf over his shoulder. I had gone to get needles, and he had come in for the bounty. Scott insisted on the whole carcass, having once been bamboozled by a Yankee who brought in a pair of ears one day and claimed his bounty, then some time later brought in the paws for another dollar, and finally the tail. It was winter and the parts looked fairly fresh, but the con became common knowledge, to Scott's disgust. So the wolf's face was the first thing I saw when I walked in. The tongue lolled out of the mouth, which was pulled back in a grimace. I flinched, despite myself. Scott yelled and Jammet apologised profusely; it was impossible to be angry with him, what with his charm and his limp. The carcass was removed out back somewhere, and as I was browsing, they began to argue about the moth-eaten pelt that hangs over the door. I think Jammet suggested jokingly that Scott replace it with a new one. The sign under it reads, 'Canis lupus (male), the first wolf to be caught in the Town of Caulfield, 11th February, 1860.' The sign tells you a lot about John Scott, demonstrating his pretensions to learning, his self-importance and the craven respect for authority over truth. It certainly wasn't the first wolf to be caught round here, and there is no such thing as the town of Caulfield, strictly speaking, although he would like there to be, because then there would be a Council, and he could be its Mayor.

'Anyway, that is a female. Males have a darker collar, and are bigger. This one is very small.'

Jammet knew what he was talking about, as he had caught more wolves than anyone else I know. He smiled, to show he meant no offence, but Scott takes offence like it is going out of fashion, and bristled.

'I suppose you remember better than I do, Mr Jammet?'

Jammet shrugged. Since he wasn't here in 1860, and since he was French, unlike the rest of us, he had to watch his step.

At this point I stepped up to the counter. 'I think it was a female, Mr Scott. The man who brought it in said her cubs howled all night. I remember it distinctly.'

And the way Scott strung up the carcass by its back legs outside the store for everyone to gawp at. I had never seen a wolf before, and I was surprised at its smallness. It hung with its nose pointing at the ground, eyes closed as if ashamed. Men mocked the carcass, and children laughed, daring each other to put their hand in its mouth. They posed with it for each other's amusement.

Scott turned tiny, bright blue eyes on me, either affronted that I should side with a foreigner, or just affronted, it was hard to tell.

'And look what happened to him.' Doc Wade, the man who brought in the bounty, drowned the following spring – as though that threw his judgement into question.

'Ah well…' Jammet shrugged and winked at me, the cheek.

Somehow – I think Scott mentioned it first – we got talking about those poor girls, as people usually do when the subject of wolves is raised. Although there are any number of unfortunate females in the world (plenty in my experience alone), around here 'those poor girls' always refers to only two – the Seton sisters, who vanished all those years ago. There were a few minutes' pleasant and pointless exchange of views that broke off suddenly when the bell rang and Mrs Knox came in. We pretended to be very interested in the buttons on the counter. Laurent Jammet took his dollar, bowed to me and Mrs Knox, and left. The bell jangled on its metal spring for a long time after he walked out.

That was all, nothing significant about it. The last time I saw him.

Laurent Jammet was our closest neighbour. Despite this, his life was a mystery to us. I used to wonder how he hunted wolves with his bad leg, and then someone told me that he baited deer meat with strychnine. The skill came in following the trail to the resulting corpse. I don't know though; that is not hunting as I see it. I know wolves have learned to stay out of range of a Winchester rifle, so they cannot be entirely stupid, but they are not so clever that they have learnt to distrust a free gift of food, and where is the merit in following a doomed creature to its end? There were other unusual things about him: long trips away from home in parts unknown; visits from dark, taciturn strangers; and brief displays of startling generosity, in sharp counterpoint to his dilapidated cabin. We knew that he was from Quebec. We knew that he was Catholic, although he did not often go to church or to confession (though he may have indulged in both during his long absences). He was polite and cheerful, although he did not have particular friends, and kept a certain distance. And he was, I dare say, handsome, with almost-black hair and eyes, and features that gave the impression of having just finished smiling, or being about to start. He treated all women with the same respectful charm, but managed not to irritate either them or their husbands. He was not married and showed no inclination to do so, but I have noticed that some men are happier on their own, especially if they are rather slovenly and irregular in their habits.

Some people attract an idle and entirely unmalicious envy. Jammet was one of those, lazy and good-natured, who seem to slide through life without toil or effort. I thought him lucky, because he did not seem to worry about those things that turn the rest of us grey. He had no grey hairs, but he had a past, which he kept mostly to himself. He imagined himself to have a future, too, I suppose, but he did not. He was perhaps forty. It was as old as he would ever get.

*

It is a Thursday morning in mid-November, about two weeks after that meeting in the store. I walk down the road from our house in a dreadful temper, planning my lecture carefully. More than likely I rehearse it aloud – one of many strange habits that are all too easy to pick up in the backwoods. The road – actually little more than a series of ruts worn by hooves and wheels – follows the river where it plunges down a series of shallow falls. Under the birches patches of moss gleam emerald in the sunlight. Fallen leaves, crystallised by the night's frost, crackle under my feet, whispering of the coming winter. The sky is an achingly clear blue. I walk quickly in my anger, head high. It probably makes me look cheerful.

Jammet's cabin sits away from the riverbank in a patch of weeds that passes for a garden. The unpeeled log walls have faded over the years until the whole thing looks grey and woolly, more like a living growth than a building. It is something from a bygone age: the door is buckskin stretched over a wooden frame, the windows glazed with oiled parchment. In winter he must freeze. It's not a place where the women of Dove River often call, and I haven't been here myself for months, but right now I have run out of places to look.

There is no smoke signal of life inside, but the door stands ajar; the buckskin stained from earthy hands. I call out, then knock on the wall. There is no reply, so I peer inside, and when my eyes have adjusted to the dimness I see Jammet, at home and, true to form, asleep on his bed at this time in the morning. I nearly walk away then, thinking there is no point waking him, but frustration makes me persevere. I haven't come all this way for nothing.

'Mr Jammet?' I start off, sounding, to my mind, irritatingly bright. 'Mr Jammet, I am so sorry to disturb you but I must ask…'

Laurent Jammet sleeps peacefully. Round his neck is the red neckerchief he wears for hunting, so that other hunters will not mistake him for a bear and shoot him. One foot protrudes off the side of the bed, in a dirty sock. His red neckerchief is on the table… I have grasped the side of the door. Suddenly, from being normal, everything has changed completely: flies hover round their late autumn feast; the red neckerchief is not round his neck, it cannot be, because it is on the table, and that means…

'Oh,' I say, and the sound shocks me in the silent cabin. 'No.'

I cling onto the door, trying not to run away, although I realise a second later I couldn't move if my life depended on it.

The redness round his neck has leaked onto the mattress from a gash. A gash. I'm panting, as though I've been running. The doorframe is the most important thing in the world right now. Without it, I don't know what I would do.

The neckerchief has not done its duty. It has failed to prevent his untimely death.

I don't pretend to be particularly brave, and in fact long ago gave up the notion that I have any remarkable qualities, but I am surprised at the calmness with which I look around the cabin. My first thought is that Jammet has destroyed himself, but Jammet's hands are empty, and there is no sign of a weapon near him. One hand dangles off the side of the bed. It does not occur to me to be afraid. I know with absolute certainty that whoever did this is nowhere near – the cabin proclaims its emptiness. Even the body on the bed is empty. There are no attributes to it now – the cheerfulness and slovenliness and skill at shooting, the generosity and callousness – they have all gone.

There is one other thing I can't help but notice, as his face is turned slightly away from me. I don't want to see it but it's there, and it confirms what I have already unwillingly accepted – that among all the things in the world that can never be known, Laurent Jammet's fate is not one of them. This is no accident, nor is it self-destruction. He has been scalped.

At length, although it is probably only a few seconds later, I pull the door closed behind me, and when I can't see him any more, I feel better. Although for the rest of the day, and for days after, my right hand aches from the violence with which I gripped the doorframe, as though I had been trying to knead the wood between my fingers, like dough.

WE LIVE IN Dove River, on the north shore of Georgian Bay. My husband and I emigrated from the Highlands of Scotland a dozen years ago, driven out like so many others. A million and a half people arrived in North America in just a few years, but despite the numbers involved, despite being so crammed into the hold of a ship that you thought there couldn't possibly be room in the New World for all these people, we fanned out from the landing stages at Halifax and Montreal like the tributaries of a river, and disappeared, every one, into the wilderness. The land swallowed us up, and was hungry for more. Hacking land out of the forest, we gave our places names that sprang from things we saw – a bird, an animal – or the names of old home towns; sentimental reminders of places that had no sentiment for us. It just goes to show you can't leave anything behind. You bring it all with you, whether you want to or not.

A dozen years ago there was nothing here but trees. The country to the north of here is a mean land that is either bog or stones, where even the willows and tamaracks cannot take hold. But near the river the soil is soft and deep, the forest around it so dark green it is almost black, and the sharp scented silence feels as deep and endless as the sky. My first reaction, when I saw it, was to burst into tears. The cariole that brought us rattled away, and the thought that, however loudly I screamed, only the wind would answer, could not be pushed away. Still, if the idea was to find peace and quiet, we had succeeded. My husband waited calmly for my fit of hysteria to subside, then said, with a grim sort of smile:

'Out here, there is nothing greater than God.'

Assuming you believe in that sort of thing, it seemed a safe bet.

In time I got used to the silence, and the thinness of the air that made everything seem brighter and sharper than it had back home. I even grew to like it. And I named it, since it had no name that anyone knew of: Dove River.

I'm not immune to sentimentality myself.

Others came. Then John Scott built the flour mill near the river mouth, and having spent so much money on it, and it having such a nice view of the bay, decided he might as well live in it. Somehow this started a fashion for living near the shore, inexplicable to those of us who had gone upriver precisely to escape the howling storms when the Bay seems to turn into an angry ocean intent on clawing back the land you have so presumptuously settled. But Caulfield (sentiment again; Scott is from Dumfriesshire) took in a way that Dove River never could – because of the abundance of level land and relative sparseness of the forest, and because Scott opened a dry goods store that made backwoods life a lot easier. Now there is a community of over a hundred – a strange mix of Scots and Yankees. And Laurent Jammet. He hasn't – hadn't – been here long, and probably would never have moved here at all had he not taken the piece of land that no one else would touch.

Four years ago he bought the farm downstream from ours. It had been lying empty for some time, on account of the previous owner, an elderly Scot. Doc Wade arrived in Dove River seeking cheap land where he would not be so much under the noses of those who judged him – he had a wealthy sister and brother-in-law in Toronto. People called him Doc, although it turned out he was not a doctor at all, just a man of culture who had not found a place in the New World that appreciated his varied but nebulous talents. Unfortunately Dove River was not the exception he was looking for. As many men have found, farming is a slow, sure way to lose your fortune, destroy your health, and break your spirit. The work was too heavy for a man of his age, and his heart was not in it. His crops failed, his pigs ran wild in the forest, his cabin roof caught fire. One evening he slipped on the rock that forms a natural jetty in front of his cabin, and was later found in the deep eddy below Horsehead Bluff (so named, with that refreshing Canadian lack of imagination, because it resembles a horse's head). It was a merciful release after his troubles, said some. Others called it a tragedy – the sort of small, domestic tragedy the bush is littered with. I suppose I imagined it differently. Wade drank, like most men. One night, when his money was gone and the whisky finished, when there was nothing left for him to do in this world, he went down to the river and watched the cold black water rushing past. I imagine he looked up at the sky, heard the mocking, indifferent voice of the forest one last time, felt the tug of the swollen river, and cast himself onto its infinite mercy.

Afterwards, local gossip said that the land was unlucky, but it was cheap enough and Jammet was not one to take note of superstitious rumours, although perhaps he should have. He had been a voyageur for the Company, and had fallen under a canoe while hauling it up some rapids. The accident lamed him, and they gave him compensation. He seemed grateful rather than otherwise for his accident, which gave him enough money to buy his own land. He was fond of saying how lazy he was, and certainly he did not do the farm work that most men cannot avoid. He sold off most of Wade's land and made his living form the wolf bounty and a little trading. Every spring a succession of dark, long-distance men would come from the northwest with their canoes and packs. They found him a congenial person to do business with.

Half an hour later I am knocking on the door of the biggest house in Caulfield. I flex the fingers of my right hand as I wait for an answer – they seem to have seized up into a sort of claw.

Mr Knox has a poor, greyish complexion that makes me think of liver salts, and is tall and thin, with a hatchet profile that seems permanently poised to strike down the unworthy – useful attributes for a magistrate. I suddenly feel as empty as if I had not eaten for a week.

'Ah, Mrs Ross… an unexpected pleasure…'

To tell the truth he looks, more than anything, alarmed at the sight of me. Perhaps he looks at everyone this way, but it gives the impression he knows slightly more about me than I would like, and thus knows I am not the sort of person he would want his daughters to associate with.

'Mr Knox… I'm afraid it is not a pleasure. There has been a… a terrible accident.'

Scenting gossip of the richest sort, Mrs Knox comes in a minute later, and I tell them both what is in the cabin by the river. Mrs Knox clutches at the little gold cross at her throat. Knox receives the news calmly, but turns away at one point, and turns back, having, I can't help feeling, composed his features into a suitable cast – grim, stern, resolute, and so on. Mrs Knox sits beside me stroking my hand while I try not to snatch it away.

'And to think, the last time I saw him was in the store that time. He looked so…'

I nod in agreement, thinking how we had fallen into a guilty silence on her approach. After many protestations of shocked sympathy and advice for shattered nerves, she rushes off to inform their two daughters in a suitable way (in other words, with far more detail than if their father were present). Knox dispatches a messenger to Fort Edgar to summon some Company men. He leaves me to admire the view, then returns to say he has summoned John Scott (who in addition to owning the store and flour mill, has several warehouses and a great deal of land) to go with him to examine the cabin and secure it against 'intrusion' until the Company representatives arrive. That is the word he uses, and I feel a certain criticism. Not that he can blame me for finding the body, but I am sure he regrets that a mere farmer's wife has sullied the scene before he has had a chance to exercise his superior faculties. But I sense something else in him too, other than his disapproval – excitement. He sees a chance for himself to shine in a drama far more urgent than most that occur in the backwoods – he is going to investigate. I presume he takes Scott so that it looks official and there is a witness to his genius, and because Scott's age and wealth give him a sort of status. It can be nothing to do with intelligence – Scott is living proof that the wealthy are not necessarily better or cleverer than the rest of us.

We head upriver in Knox's trap. Since Jammet's cabin is close to our house, they cannot avoid my accompanying them, and since we reach his cabin first, I offer to come in with them. Knox wrinkles his brow with avuncular concern.

'You must be exhausted after your terrible shock. I insist that you go home and rest.'

'We will be able to see whatever you saw,' Scott adds. And more, is the implication.

I turn away from Scott – there is no point arguing with some people – and address the hatchet profile. He is affronted, I realise, that my feminine nature can bear the thought of confronting such horror again. But something inside me hardens stubbornly against his assumption that he and only he will draw the right conclusions. Or perhaps it is just that I don't like being told what to do. I say I can tell them if anything has been disturbed, which they cannot deny, and anyway, short of manhandling me down the track and locking me in my house, there is little they can do.

The autumn weather is being kind, but there is the faint tang of decay when Knox pulls open the door. I didn't notice it before. Knox steps forward, breathing through his mouth and puts his fingers on Jammet's hand – I see him hover, wondering where to touch him – before pronouncing him quite cold. The two men speak in low voices, almost whispering. I understand – to speak louder would be rude. Scott takes out a notebook and writes down what Knox says as he observes the position of the body, the temperature of the stove, the arrangement of items in the room. Then Knox stands for a while doing nothing, but still manages to look purposeful – an accident of anatomy I observe with interest. There is a scuff of footprints on the dusty floor, but no strange objects, no weapon of any sort. The only clue is that awful round wound on Jammet's head. It must have been an Indian outlaw, Knox says. Scott agrees: no white man could do something so barbaric. I picture his wife's face last winter, when it was swollen black and blue and she claimed he had slipped on a patch of ice, although everybody knew the truth.

The men go upstairs to the other room. I can tell where they go by the creak of their feet pressing on floorboards and the dust that falls between them and catches the light. It trickles onto Jammet's corpse, falling softly on this cheek, like snowflakes. Little flecks land, unbearably, on his open eyes and I can't take my gaze off them. I have an urge to go and brush it off, tell them sharply to stop disturbing things, but I don't do either. I can't make myself touch him.

'No one has been up there for days – the dust was quite undisturbed,' says Knox when they are down again, flicking dirt off their trousers with pocket-handkerchiefs. Knox has brought a clean sheet from upstairs, and he shakes it out, sending more dust motes whirling round the room like a swarm of sunlit bees. He places the sheet over the body on the bed.

'There, that should keep the flies off,' he says with an air of self-congratulation, though any fool can see that it will do no such thing.

It is decided that we – or rather they – can do no more, and on leaving, Knox closes and secures the door with a length of wire with a blob of sealing wax. A detail that, though I hate to admit it, impresses me.

RESTLESS

by **William Boyd**

BLOOMSBURY

RESTLESS

by **William Boyd**

During the long, hot summer of 1976, Ruth Gilmartin discovers that her very English mother Sally is really Eva Delectorskaya, a Russian émigrée and one-time spy. In 1939, Eva is a beautiful 28-year-old living in Paris. As war breaks out, she is recruited for the British Secret Service by Lucas Romer, a mysterious, patrician Englishman. Under his tutelage she learns to become the perfect spy, to mask her emotions and trust no one.

William Boyd *was born in Accra, Ghana and is the author of eight previous novels, many of which have won prizes - including A Good Man in Africa which won the Whitbread First Novel Award in 1981. A former television critic for the New Statesman, Boyd is also a scriptwriter. Some thirteen of his screenplays have been filmed and in 1998 he both wrote and directed the feature film, The Trench. William Boyd lives in London and was awarded the CBE in 2005.*

"Restless remains in the mind long after you finish it. All rests precariously on double crosses and double bluffs, even for the reader. Wartime tension, the smell of espionage, and the consequences of deceitful lives are played out with effortless clarity, resulting in an unputdownable read."

Judges
Kate Adie – Author and Broadcaster
Susie Dent – Writer and Broadcaster on language
Mike Gayle – Author and Journalist

RESTLESS

for Susan

We may, indeed, say that the hour of death is uncertain, but when we say this we think of that hour as situated in a vague and remote expanse of time; it does not occur to us that it can have any connection with the day that has already dawned and can mean that death may occur this very afternoon, so far from uncertain, this afternoon whose timetable, hour by hour, has been settled in advance. One insists on one's daily outing, so that in a month's time one will have had the necessary ration of fresh air; one has hesitated over which coat to take, which cabman to call; one is in the cab, the whole day lies before one, short because one must be back home early, as a friend is coming to see one; one hopes it will be as fine again tomorrow; and one has no suspicion that death, which has been advancing within one on another plane, has chosen precisely this particular day to make its appearance in a few minutes' time . . .
Marcel Proust, *The Guermantes Way*

I

INTO THE HEART OF ENGLAND

WHEN I WAS A child and was being fractious and contrary and generally behaving badly, my mother used to rebuke me by saying: 'One day someone will come and kill me and then you'll be sorry'; or, 'They'll appear out of the blue and whisk me away – how would you like that?'; or, 'You'll wake up one morning and I'll be gone. Disappeared. You wait and see.'

It's curious, but you don't think seriously about these remarks when you're young. But now – as I look back on the events of that interminable hot summer of 1976, that summer when England reeled, gasping for breath, pole-axed by the unending heat – now

I know what my mother was talking about: I understand that bitter dark current of fear that flowed beneath the placid surface of her ordinary life – how it had never left her even after years of peaceful, unexceptional living. I now realise she was always frightened that someone was going to come and kill her. And she had good reason.

It all started, I remember, in early June. I can't recall the exact day – a Saturday, most likely, because Jochen wasn't at his nursery school – and we both drove over to Middle Ashton as usual. We took the main road out of Oxford to Stratford and then turned off it at Chipping Norton, heading for Evesham, and then we turned off again and again, as if we were following a descending scale of road types; trunk road, road, B-road, minor road, until we found ourselves on the metalled cart track that led through the dense and venerable beech wood down to the narrow valley that contained the tiny village of Middle Ashton. It was a journey I made at least twice a week and each time I did so I felt I was being led into the lost heart of England – a green, forgotten, inverse Shangri-La where everything became older, mouldier and more decrepit.

Middle Ashton had grown up, centuries ago, around the Jacobean manor house – Ashton House – at its centre, still occupied by a distant relative of the original owner-builder-proprietor, one Trefor Parry, a seventeenth-century Welsh wool-merchant-made-good, who, flaunting his great wealth, had built his grand demesne here in the middle of England itself. Now, after generation upon generation of reckless, spendthrift Parrys and their steadfast, complacent neglect, the manor house was falling down, on its last woodwormed legs, giving up its parched ghost to entropy. Sagging tarpaulins covered the roof of the east wing, rusting scaffolding spoke of previous vain gestures at restoration and the soft yellow Cotswold stone of its walls came away in your hand like wet toast. There was a small damp dark church near by, overwhelmed by massive black-green yews that seemed to drink the light of day; a cheerless pub – the Peace and Plenty, where the hair on your head brushed the greasy, nicotine varnish of the ceiling in the bar – a post office with a shop and an off-license, and a scatter of cottages, some thatched, green with moss, and interesting old houses in big gardens. The lanes in the village were sunk six feet beneath high banks with rampant hedges growing on either side, as if the traffic of ages past, like a river, had eroded the road into its own mini-valley, deeper and deeper, a foot each decade. The oaks, the beeches, the chestnuts were towering, hoary old ancients, casting the village in a kind of permanent gloaming during the day and in the night providing an atonal symphony of creaks and groans, whispers and sighs as the night breezes shifted the massive branches and the old wood moaned and complained.

I was looking forward to Middle Ashton's generous shade as it was another blearily hot day – every day seemed hot, that summer – but we weren't yet bored to oblivion by the heat. Jochen was in the back, looking out of the car's rear window – he liked to see the road 'unwinding', he said. I was listening to music on the radio when I heard him ask me a question.

'If you speak to a window I can't hear you,' I said.

'Sorry, Mummy.'

He turned himself and rested his elbows on my shoulders and I heard his quiet voice in my ear.

'Is Granny your real mummy?'

'Of course she is, why?'

'I don't know . . . She's so strange.'

'Everybody's strange when you come to think of it,' I said. 'I'm strange . . . You're strange . . .'

'That's true,' he said, 'I know.' He set his chin on my shoulder and dug it down, working the muscle above my right collar-bone with his little pointed chin, and I felt tears smart in my eyes. He did this to me from time to time, did Jochen, my strange son – and made me want to cry for annoying reasons I couldn't really explain.

At the entrance to the village, opposite the grim pub, the Peace and Plenty, a brewer's lorry was parked, delivering beer. There was the narrowest of gaps for the car to squeeze through.

'You'll scrape Hippo's side,' Jochen warned. My car was a

seventh-hand Renault 5, sky blue with a (replaced) crimson bonnet. Jochen has wanted to christen it and I had said that because it was a French car we should give it a French name and so I suggested Hippolyte (I had been reading Taine, for some forgotten scholarly reason) and so 'Hippo' it became – at least to Jochen. I personally can't stand people who give their cars names.

'No, I won't,' I said. 'I'll be careful.'

I had just about negotiated my way through, inching by, when the driver of the lorry, I supposed, appeared from the pub, strode into the gap and histrionically waved me on. He was a youngish man with a big gut straining his sweatshirt and distorting its Morrell's logo and his bright beery face boasted mutton-chop whiskers a Victorian dragoon would have been proud of.

'Come on, come on, yeah, yeah, you're all right, darling,' he wheedled tiredly at me, his voice heavy with a weary exasperation. 'It's not a bloody Sherman tank.'

As I came level with him I wound down the window and smiled.

I said: 'If you'd get your fat gut out of the way it'd be a whole lot easier, you fucking arsehole.'

I accelerated off before he could collect himself and wound up the window again, feeling my anger evaporate – deliciously, tinglingly – as quickly as it had surged up. I was not in the best of moods, true, because, as I was attempting to hang a poster in my study that morning, I had, with cartoonish inevitability and ineptitude, hit my thumbnail – which was steadying the picture hook – square on with the hammer instead of the nail of the picture hook. Charlie Chaplin would have been proud of me as I squealed and hopped and flapped my hand as if I wanted to shake it off my wrist. My thumbnail, beneath its skin-coloured plaster, was now a damson purple, and a little socket of pain located in my thumb throbbed with my pulse like some sort of organic timepiece, counting down the seconds of my mortality. But as we accelerated away I could sense the adrenalin-charged heart-thud, the head-reel of pleasure at my audacity: at moments like this I felt I knew all the latent anger buried in me – in me and in our species.

'Mummy, you used the F-word,' Jochen said, his voice softened with stern reproach.

'I'm sorry, but that man really annoyed me.'

'He was only trying to help.'

'No, he wasn't. He was trying to patronise me.'

Jochen sat and considered this new word for a while, then gave up.

'Here we are at last,' he said.

My mother's cottage sat amidst dense, thronging vegetation surrounded by an unclipped, undulating box hedge that was thick with rambling roses and clematis. Its tufty hand-shorn lawn was an indecent moist green, an affront to the implacable sun. From the air, I thought, the cottage and its garden must look like a verdant oasis, its shaggy profusion in this hot summer almost challenging the authorities to impose an immediate hosepipe ban. My mother was an enthusiastic and idiosyncratic gardener: she planted close and pruned hard. If a plant or bush flourished she let it go, not worrying if it stifled others or cast inappropriate shade. Her garden, she claimed, was designed to be a controlled wilderness – she did not own a mower, she cut her lawn with shears – and she knew it annoyed others in the village where neatness and order were the pointed and visible virtues. But none could argue or complain that her garden was abandoned or unkempt: no one in the village spent more time in her garden than Mrs Sally Gilmartin and the fact that her industry was designed to create lushness and wildness was something that could be criticised, perhaps, but not condemned.

We called it a cottage but in fact it was a small two-storey ashlar house in sandy Cotswold stone with a flint tiled roof, rebuilt in the eighteenth century. The upper floor had kept its older mullioned windows, the bedrooms were dark and low, whereas the ground floor had sash windows and a handsome carved doorway with fluted half-columns and a scrolled pediment. She had somehow managed to buy it from Huw Parry-Jones, the dipsomaniac owner of Ashton House, when he was more than particularly hard up, and its rear backed on to the modest remnants of Ashton House park – now an uncut and uncropped meadow – all that was left of the thousands of rolling acres that the Parry family had originally owned in this part of Oxfordshire. To one side was a wooden shed-cum-garage almost completely overwhelmed by ivy and Virginia creeper. I saw her car was parked there – a white Austin Allegro – so I knew she was at home.

Jochen and I opened the gate and looked around for her, Jochen calling, 'Granny, we're here,' and being answered by a loud 'Hip-hip hooray!' coming from the rear of the house. And then she appeared, wheeling herself along the brick path in a wheelchair. She stopped and held out her arms as if to scoop us into her embrace, but we both stood there, immobile, astonished.

'Why on earth are you in a wheelchair?' I said. 'What's happened?'

'Push me inside, dear,' she said. 'All shall be revealed.'

As Jochen and I wheeled her inside, I noticed there was a little wooden ramp up to the front step.

'How long have you been like this, Sal?' I asked. 'You should have called me.'

'Oh, two, three days,' she said, 'nothing to worry about.'

I wasn't feeling the concern that perhaps I should have experienced because my mother looked so patently well: her face lightly tanned, her thick grey-blond hair lustrous and recently cut. And, as if to confirm this impromptu diagnosis, once we had bumped her inside she stepped out of her wheelchair and stooped easily to give Jochen a kiss.

'I fell,' she said, gesturing at the staircase. 'The last two or three steps – tripped, fell to the ground and hurt my back. Doctor Thorne suggested I got a wheelchair to cut down on my walking. Walking makes it worse, you see.'

'Who's Doctor Thorne? What happened to Doctor Brotherton?'

'On holiday. Thorne's the locum. Was the locum.' She paused. 'Nice young man. He's gone now.'

She led us through to the kitchen. I looked for evidence of a bad back in her gait and posture but could see nothing.

'It does help, really,' she said, as if she could sense my growing bafflement, my scepticism. 'The wheelchair, you know, for pottering about. It's amazing how much time one spends on one's feet in a day.'

Jochen opened the fridge. 'What's for lunch, Granny?' he asked.

'Salad,' she said. 'Too hot to cook. Help yourself to a drink, darling.'

'I love salad,' Jochen said, reaching for a can of Coca-Cola. 'I like cold food best.'

'Good boy.' My mother drew me aside. 'I'm afraid he can't stay this afternoon. I can't manage with the wheelchair and whatnot.'

I concealed my disappointment and my selfish irritation – Saturday afternoons on my own, while Jochen spent half the day at Middle Ashton, had become precious to me. My mother walked to the window, and shaded her eyes to peer out. Her kitchen/dining-room looked over her garden and her garden backed on to the meadow that was cut very haphazardly, sometimes with a gap of two or three years, and as a result was full of wild flowers and myriad types of grass and weed. And beyond the meadow was the wood, called Witch Wood for some forgotten reason – ancient woodland of oak, beech and chestnut, all the elms gone, or going, of course. There was something very odd happening here, I said to myself: something beyond my mother's usual whims and cultivated eccentricities. I went up to her and placed my hand reassuringly on her shoulder.

'Is everything all right, old thing?'

'Mmm. It was just a fall. A shock to the system, as they say. I should be fine again in a week or two.'

'There's nothing else, is there? You would tell me . . .'

She turned her handsome face on me and gave me her famous candid stare, the pale blue eyes wide – I knew it well. But I could face it out, now, these days, after everything I'd been through myself: I wasn't so cowed by it anymore.

'What else could it be, my darling? Senile dementia?'

All the same, she asked me to wheel her in her wheelchair

through the village to the post office to buy a needless pint of milk and pick up a newspaper. She talked at some length about her bad back to Mrs Cumber, the postmistress, and made me stop on the return journey to converse over a drystone wall with Percy Fleet, the young local builder, and his long-term girlfriend (Melinda? Melissa?) as they waited for their barbecue to heat up – a brick edifice with a chimney set proudly on the paving in front of their new conservatory. They commiserated: a fall was the worst thing. Melinda recalled an old stroke-ridden uncle who'd been shaken up for weeks after he'd slipped in the bathroom.

'I want one of those, Percy,' my mother said, pointing at the conservatory, 'very fine.'

'Free estimates, Mrs Gilmartin.'

'How was your aunt? Did she enjoy herself?'

'My mother-in-law,' Percy corrected.

'Ah yes, of course. It was your mother-in-law.'

We said our goodbyes and I pushed her wearily on over the uneven surface of the lane, feeling a growing itch of anger at being asked to take part in this pantomime. She was always commenting on comings and goings too, as if she were checking on people, clocking them on and clocking them off like some obsessive foreman checking on his work-force – she'd done this as long as I could remember. I told myself to be calm: we would have lunch, I would take Jochen back to the flat, he could play in the garden, we could go for a walk in the University Parks . . .

'You mustn't be angry with me, Ruth,' she said, glancing back at me over her shoulder.

I stopped pushing and took out and lit a cigarette. 'I'm not angry.'

'Oh, yes you are. Just let me see how I cope. Perhaps next Saturday I'll be fine.'

When we came in Jochen said darkly, after a minute, 'You can get cancer from cigarettes, you know.' I snapped at him and we ate our lunch in a rather tense mood of long silences broken by bright banal observations about the village on my mother's part. She persuaded me to have a glass of wine and I began to relax. I helped her wash up and stood drying the dishes beside her as she rinsed the glasses in hot water. Water-daughter, daughter-water, sought her daughter in the water, I rhymed to myself, suddenly glad it was the weekend, with no teaching, no tutees and thinking it was maybe not such a bad thing to be spending some time alone with my son. Then my mother said something.

She was shading her eyes again, looking out at the wood.

'What?'

'Can you see someone? Is there someone in the wood?'

I peered. 'Not that I can spot. Why?'

'I thought I saw someone.'

'Ramblers, picnickers – it's Saturday, the sun is shining.'

'Oh yes, that's right: the sun is shining and all is well with the world.'

She went to the dresser and picked up a pair of binoculars she kept there and turned to focus them on the wood.

I ignored her sarcasm and went to find Jochen and we prepared to leave. My mother took her seat in her wheelchair and pointedly wheeled it to the front door. Jochen told the story of the encounter with the driver of the brewer's lorry and my unashamed use of the F-word. My mother cupped his face with her hands and smiled at him, adoringly.

'Your mother can get very angry when she wants to and no doubt that man was very stupid,' she said. 'Your mother is a very angry young woman.'

'Thank you for that, Sal,' I said and bent to kiss her forehead. 'I'll call this evening.'

'Would you do me a little favour?' she said and then asked me if, when I telephoned in future, I would let the phone ring twice, then hang up and ring again. 'That way I'll know it's you,' she explained. 'I'm not so fast about the house in the chair.'

Now, for the first time I felt a real small pang of worry: this request did seem to be the sign of some initial form of derangement or delusion – but she caught the look in my eye.

'I know what you're thinking, Ruth,' she said. 'But you're quite wrong, quite wrong.' She stood up out of her chair, tall and rigid.

'Wait a second,' she said and went upstairs.

'Have you made Granny cross again?' Jochen said, in a low voice, accusingly.

'No.'

My mother came down the stairs – effortlessly, it seemed to me – carrying a thick buff folder under her arm. She held it out for me.

'I'd like you to read this,' she said.

I took it from her. There seemed to be some dozens of pages – different types, different sizes of paper. I opened it. There was a title page: The Story of Eva Delectorskaya.

'Eva Delectorskaya,' I said, mystified. 'Who's that?'

'Me,' she said. 'I am Eva Delectorskaya.'

KEEPING MUM

by **Brian Thompson**

KEEPING MUM

by **Brian Thompson**

Mum and Dad – Squibs and Bert – were a complete mystery to Brian Thompson as he grew up in Cambridge and London during the 1940s. His mother danced with the Yanks all night and slept under a fake fur coat all day. When his father bothered to come home he resolutely discouraged Brian in everything. Other children were evacuated out of the big cities, but Brian found himself travelling in to the capital. He spent much of the Blitz with an eccentric swarm of relations whose geography was the street, the pub, the market and two or three useful tramlines. Brian was snatched from his working-class roots by the Butler Act of 1944 and given an education that would lead to Cambridge University, books, pipe-smoking and rose trellises.

Brian Thompson *was born in Lambeth, London in 1935. He undertook national service in Kenya and taught in secondary and adult education for 15 years. Since 1973 he has written for a living as a radio and television playwright and documentary film maker. He is also the author of several acclaimed biographies and seven stage plays. He currently lives in Oxford.*

"This vivid, life-affirming and deftly-written book is a perfect antidote to the 'misery memoir'. We defy anyone not to enjoy it."

Judges
Hazel Broadfoot – Co-Owner, Village Books (Dulwich)
Sean O'Hagan – Writer, The Observer
Francis Wheen – Author and Biographer

KEEPING MUM

For Clare

CHAPTER ONE

I AM ON MY STOMACH, HALF ACROSS MY MOTHER'S body. Her skin smells of sleep and – by association – milk. Downstairs, the front door slams. My mother pushes me away and rolls on to her side. Her hair fans out on the pillow and though she is facing the light that streams through uncurtained windows, her eyes are closed. There are tears in her lashes. She is not sleeping but crying. After a few moments, I clamber out of bed.

Maybe I was three, maybe younger. If three, it was the year Hitler assumed the office of war minister and Neville Chamberlain went to see him at Berchtesgaden. A fortnight later, at the end of September 1938, Chamberlain and the French chief minister Edouard Daladier were summoned to Munich to sign an infamous agreement with the Führer and Mussolini. Though I had no way of knowing it, things might have been worse. I might have been born Czech, or even more calamitously as it proved in the end, German. As it was, the sunlight that streamed into the bedroom illuminated a complacent, apolitical family home. Not a happy home, not in the slightest bit happy; but then, what people did with themselves was their own business. This widely shared belief was what gave these bricks and mortar their Englishness.

My father went to work early in order to impress the bosses – but that was just his way. The rest of the road tramped off half an hour later to clerks' desks or jobs in shops, to college kitchens or inspection pits in oily garages. Their wives set about the washing or cleaning; at the end of the morning they stood on chairs to gossip across the garden fences. My mother did little of any of these things but that too was just her way. For her, the world was huge and for the most part shapeless. We had gone up in it by coming to live here, but only in the way a bubble rises from the marsh. Some would say she did not know how lucky she was. The rented house we lived in was modern and the road lined with generous grass verges. Every so often a tree had been planted along the way to add grace and scale and as it happened there was one outside our house, showering blossom in spring. It made no difference to my mother. Those early-morning tears came from something much more deep and dark and incoherent than disappointment with her surroundings.

The back garden of the house was bounded on three sides by high cedarwood fences and had for its lid a milky-blue sky, vaster than anything we could have imagined possible in London. There, in the Victorian canyons of my parents' childhood, the sky was like a piece of fabric cut up in narrow strips and stuffed to fill a crack or stop a draught. In the crowded streets no gutter was without its stalking, strutting pigeons. Rats whose ancestors had seen the Romans plopped down the drains or scratted in the ceiling. The flinty yellow brick of houses and tenements was black with soot and even a little sunshine revealed how dense the air was with dust and grit. Victorian – Dickensian – factories and workshops stood alongside dwellings: yards away from my father's birthplace was a marble-cutting business worked in the open air, the steam-driven saws sending up fogs of fine white powder. My mother had grown up next door to rag-pickers.

Now, in place of all that, a yawning sky, blustery keen air and rain so fresh that it seemed to improve the washing on the line. While my mother's best scorn was reserved for the people she had left behind, her vandalism soon found its full outlet under such an all-seeing eye. She would walk across the chalky borders of the garden and stamp down shows of spring daffodils, or dash the dregs of her tea into the rose bushes, scattering petals. On hot days she would sit on a chair outside the kitchen door, her legs exposed to the crotch of her knickers, her back turned resolutely to the pleasures of the lawn, smoking and throwing the dog-ends at the dustbin. Though she was hardly thirty years old, she dressed like someone twenty or even forty years older, a bundle of garish rags and lumpy cardigans. Congenitally hard of hearing, when she was not being badgered by someone else's speech her expression assumed a startling emptiness. She was inside there somewhere, but on her own.

My father made the transition to the country more easily by playing the part of bluff yeoman. He was in fact a telephone linesman, shrewdly aware that he had joined the most meritocratic branch of the civil service, as Post Office Engineering was in those days. Climbing up telephone poles was merely a way of looking round to see how the land lay. He was ruthlessly ambitious and a quick learner. He already had two voices, one more polite than the other. When he bought shoes, they were brogues. His shirts were check and his jackets sporty. He took himself off every Sunday for what he liked to call a walk round the parish. By the standards of the times he lived in, he was exceptionally good-looking, with a straight nose inherited from his mother and a burly no-nonsense figure, honed by childhood boxing. He wore his moustache clipped in the manner of Clark Gable and smoked both cigarettes and a pipe.

The pipe gave him a curiously authoritative air, as of a young British bulldog, a man of dangerous parts. Although we had come no further than fifty miles from London, men in his mould were scattered all over the dying Empire, implacable and incorruptible. He was exactly the sort of stout fellow who would know what to do when the drums fell silent and the house servants slipped away out of the compound. Instead of the unblinking animosity of the jungle, however, he had a crazy wife and a skinny child, a rented house and a hundred feet or so of chalky mud.

Though this was still a very young garden, it sagged in the middle like a ruined sofa. That same soft curve was replicated by a rose trellis that had already begun to bow for lack of support. The laths were whimsically coated in flaky and weathered blue distemper, a colour to be found inside the house on the bathroom walls. How to explain this oddity, except as an example of my father's restless and chippy individualism, his gift for doing whatever the hell he liked with the material world? The man next door, a retired policeman, explained in a slow country voice how there were special creosotes that could be used on such a thing as a trellis. This conversation took place over a boundary fence. My father simply stared his neighbour down with his pale blue eyes.

'Suit yourself,' Mr Blundell muttered unnecessarily, as his head disappeared from view.

For miles round was chalk. Wherever a section had been cut, say to accommodate a road through the soft and rounded hills, stiff grey topsoil perched like breadcrumbs on the altar of grubby white. There were cliffs of the stuff in forgotten woodland spinneys, stained green by gouts of winter rain. Only half a mile away along the same reef on which our house had been built was a cement works which mined chalk from two huge holes in the ground, connected to each other by a subterranean tunnel. The mixing tank, in which an iron sweep rotated day and night, had a blackboard fastened to its crusty wall. It showed the number of days that had passed without an industrial accident.

My father's mind was baffled by it all. His childhood had been spent looking out on to a small flagged yard with a mangle shed and an outside privy, the only view the upper three walkways of a Peabody building. The yard was bounded by a high brick wall topped with the brown glass of broken beer bottles. It helps explain my father's character. Otherness – not all, but most – was the enemy of his childhood and all his life he retained a truculence towards other people that could be truly awesome. In his world, nobody acted from a disinterested motive. All vicars were poofs, all policemen bent as meat-hooks. Even the most prestigious shops would rook you if they could and in humbler transactions it was imperative to check change for foreign coin. A kind word disguised a sinister intention and to be asked directions in the street was the obvious prelude to begging. It made him a mean-minded man. He learned how to dissimulate to his office superiors, but at the family hearth his suspicious mind was given full rein. Even at his death, some fifty years into the future, he was still living behind walls topped by broken glass.

All the same, in this new place he had found for himself, he gave the countryside every chance to seduce him. He bought a spindly and cumbersome pushchair and in this he would walk me to Cherry Hinton, then a bucolic village decorated with straw wisps. Horse-drawn drays delivered beer to the ivy-covered pub, the horses with ribbons plaited in their manes. Always interested in how things worked, my father would bid me watch as the barrels rolled off the dray, cushioned by a huge sack of sawdust, before disappearing down a steel-hooped ladder into the cellar. I seem to remember a track or path that led back down to the cement works, where he would stand, smoking, sometimes holding me up to watch the cement being mixed. Nearby, men coated in grey dust from head to toe sat on the steps of a small green cabin, watching my father watching them. They gargled water from black screw-top bottles and spat it out in silver gouts.

The painted trellis in our garden, the geometric borders, formed a sketch of what someone recently coming into the country would consider a lovesome thing – but it was only a sketch, the roughest of drafts. The chalk mocked the Adam in my father. Some of the chunks his spade turned up were as large as house bricks. His one great success was in the front garden, where a hedge of lavender ran away with itself so successfully that in the summer season brown-faced gipsies would plunder it, breaking off the stems with a blackened thumbnail, before being repelled by my mother with lumps of chalk. They left behind a scribbled mark on the gatepost, which was bad luck to receive but even worse luck to wash off. An Irishwoman a few doors down came to inspect the mark and hastily crossed herself.

'Your bleeding relatives, I shouldn't wonder,' my mother jeered.

The houses on the opposite side of the road were of an older stock. Once, our more established neighbours had been able to stand in their front rooms, which they no doubt called the sitting room, gazing out from their bow windows on to nature. Now, instead of rooks on sentry-go or ponies stirred to a gallop by some trick of the wind, they had us. Next door but one was a gap in the housing row where one day a side road would be built and more houses added, right up to the borders of a commercial apple orchard. At the end of the road, two massive billboards advertised this promise. We ingrates were the forerunners of 'Homes for the Future'.

I always imagine some architect laying down his pencil on the final drawings of this development and finding them good. Another boat sent out into the ocean of opportunity, another chance for the man in the street to rise to the challenge of the street's design. The Homes for the Future depicted on the advertising hoarding showed a family of cyclists pedalling towards the viewer – mother, father and young boy. They were laughing for joy.

It is a rainy spring day in 1940. I am collecting nuggets of slimy chalk when my father comes out of the back door and, pointing to a Tiger Moth wobbling towards Marshall's airfield, in a weeping sky, asks me whether I noticed him earlier, waving to me. I stare at the plane and mild panic in my expression amuses him.

'You didn't see me?' he persists. 'I could see you plain as anything.'

'What was I doing?'

'Picking your nose, as usual.'

I can locate this fateful little conversation exactly, to the last white snail hanging on a blade of grass. We were three yards from the back wall of the house, in front of savagely pruned roses. My father smoked as certain actors did then, dragging the cigarette from his lips with calculated and manly vigour. I knew so very little about him but I did, tender though I was, sense a mood of danger behind the bantering.

In fact, he was giving me his Clark Gable. My mother (a rather crazed Vivien Leigh) joined us with two flowered tea-cups. There was much more of this suppressed danger in the adult conversation that followed. I utterly failed to register the importance of what was being said and wandered away. This, as I can see now – only too clearly – was a mistake. When I looked up again, they had gone inside. Soon, what had been promised arrived. The shouting began and there was the sound of breaking crockery. Perfectly secure in a reserved occupation, with only his garden to think about, my father had gone out that morning and volunteered for RAF aircrew.

I must have been in the first year at school. I can remember the name of it – Blinco Grove Primary – but very little else. It seems to me I was only there for a day, during which we played some outdoor game-in-a-circle with a scuffed yellow ball and then were put down on cots to sleep for half an hour or so. I can recall the dust-impregnated blankets and the faintly sour smell of the boarded floor but not a single lesson, nor anyone's name. By stretching my memory to the limit, I can vaguely remember being given Canadian chocolate compressed into a brick inches thick. Was that then, or later?

The route home from school lay through a street of villas that had donated their railings to the war effort, leaving behind soft plugs of lead in the low walls. You turned into the main road by a parade dominated by a fish and chip shop and then crunched across a kind of clinker court to a broad pavement. To people I met along the way, I was some lallygagging freak, a thin and pigeon-chested child who had betrayed the promise shown in my only photograph to date, where I sat plumped in a chair, looking sullen and clutching a toy horse.

There was a man halfway along this road home who sometimes passed the time of day. I was peering into his hedge one afternoon when he came out of his front door, his watery eyes lighting at once on what I was looking at.

'It's a bumblebee,' he said.

'I know.'

'Ah, you know that much, do you?'

We studied each other. The bags under the man's eyes were dark blue, a colour heightened by white stubble and flyaway hair. There was food caked to his chin. He nodded, as if in answer to an unspoken question.

'Yes,' he said. 'I'm doolally.'

I told him my name.

'That's no name for a hero. Don't you want to be a hero?'

At which his daughter came out and shepherded him wordlessly back into the house. The door slammed with enough force to make the knocker clack. I did not know whether I wanted to be a hero and crossed the road with tears in my eyes. Blubbing was something to feel guilty about, like physical imperfection or dimwittedness. On her best days there could be no one more inventively ribald than my mother, yet the slightest sign of turmoil in others plunged her at once into black despair. It was always better to dissemble in front of her.

In the front room was a revolving bookcase, the improbable first prize in a whist tournament at which my father had of course triumphed. It carried *Newne's Encyclopaedia of Gardening* and nothing else. If, when it was spun, the shelf containing the encyclopaedia came to rest facing the door, Vivien Leigh would be in a merry mood. If not, there would be trouble. I sat on the rag rug, spinning the shelves and thinking about the man called Doolally and what he was doing, whether he was having his tea. There was the sudden smell of scent in the hallway and my mother came in with what she called jam doorsteps. She put the plate down beside me and checked her hair in the mirror, humming.

'I'm just going to pop out for an hour,' she said, far too casually.

My father had already gone. Though I hardly knew him, it seems significant to me now that I didn't miss him more. Without him, the house had taken on a different character. There was no more shouting. The radio was tuned to dance music, tea was sweetened with jam and when the last of the coal was used up, my mother slept inside a fake fur coat, the bedclothes heaped up in a pyramid. When she remembered, she would obligingly warm my sheets with hot water inside a Tizer bottle. Like her, I slept in my clothes. As for the garden, it reverted all too quickly to what it had been before we came there, the borders indistinguishable from the lawn, the lawn itself a tiny meadow.

I spent a great deal of time alone in the house, licking the salty grime from the window and looking down the road to watch for my mother's return from wherever she had been. Between five and six the neighbours passed, trudging home from work. By eight, the pavements were deserted. There was very little traffic and no one we knew had a car, or had ever owned one. When it had been dark an hour or so, with nothing but the wind left in the street, I would take myself off to bed. All the interior woodwork in the house was painted chocolate brown and it seemed to soak up the light furnished by low-watt bulbs. For fear of the dark, I would leave the landing light on. Flushing the lavatory also helped, for then I could fall asleep listening to the cistern grumbling and muttering to itself.

Not to be able to sleep brought on an agony of terror. My parents had given me the back bedroom, not much smaller than their own. Beyond the high fences, the branches of the commercial apple orchard chattered. It was from this direction I imagined the Germans would come, appearing out of the trees like smoke. If not Germans, then ghosts. Alone for too long, I could hear much more than the sighing all houses make when the last light is extinguished. Boots scraped along floors and there was music and the distant hum of voices. Sometimes, having put myself to bed, I heard gunshots.

'That's right,' my mother said with her elaborate sarcasm. 'That's exactly what you did hear. We was all shooting each other. The corpses are buried in Lord Muck's garden.'

'Who's Lord Muck?'

'Work it out for yourself.'

Cambridge was simply a town. The colleges had no place on my map, which was centred on Drummer Street bus and coach station. After 1942, the streets were stiff with Yanks, ambling along with wide shoes and cocky linen hats, their hands in their pockets. They looked fitter and cleaner than the miserable bundles of khaki they occasionally encountered.

'It is usual to salute an officer in this country,' I heard an elderly captain complain to three airmen young enough to be his children.

'Damn right,' some waistgunner or bombardier replied without malice, pushing him gently aside as though he were a rose sucker in our garden.

'Bloody Yanks,' the captain yelled after them, voicing the common opinion.

Then, suddenly, I am sixty miles away in another school, no more than three or four dusty rooms beside an elevated suburban railway station, learning copperplate handwriting, doing simple addition and subtraction and (for suspiciously long periods) drawing on ragged sheets of sugar paper with a thick and greasy pencil. The teachers are surely unqualified: what kind of a place is this, with its whispering somnolence, more like a Mexican hotel lounge than a classroom? I cannot see on to the station platform because it is masked by advertising hoardings, though these do not reach completely to the ground and disembodied legs occasionally walk past, pause, or in cold weather, stamp. The arrival of the trains make the nailed-down sash windows of the schoolroom shudder, a friendly and somehow reassuring whisper from the world outside.

My mother and father have disappeared and I am living with Elsie, my mother's sister. I have no more idea of how this happened than a parcel might have of the workings of the Post Office. It is the first of many holes in my memory. Was I sent away in anger, or for my own protection? Cambridge was one of the safer places to live during the war: who thought up the bright idea of posting me to a house behind the Kingston bypass, ten miles from the epicentre of the Blitz?

Here I am at eight years old, walking to school in New Malden and collecting pearly cobwebs from the suburban hedges with a twig doubled over into a hoop. In the basement of the church building that houses the school, a girl pulls down her knickers and holds up her brown gingham dress to show me what she looks like. She looks plump and well-fed, with a little pot belly and round thighs. She draws attention to a birthmark on her haunch in the shape of a Spitfire. We stand in carbolic-smelling gloom staring at each other, flinching from time to time as snatches of conversation from the street outside seem to fall through a tiled shaft and its grating. I realise what this girl expects in return. I unbutton my shorts before pulling them down to my knees. She doubles over in disbelieving laughter before running away.

She has a friend called Phyllis, a skinny carrotty girl who wears fair-isle mittens in winter. Even the dewdrop on the end of her nose is lovable to me as we walk part of the way home together. She has a neighing laugh and an inability to look me straight in the eye. My aunt and Phyllis's mother confer in Timothy White's, staring at us both from time to time with pursed lips. Uncle Dick is given the job of explaining to me how things are. Phyllis's father is Missing in Action.

'Which means he is more than likely a gonner, see? So maybe it's best to leave the poor little mite alone.'

'I haven't done anything.'

'Course not. Never said you had. But, you know, sleeping dogs. Something like that.'

Dick had one leg much shortened and wore a surgical boot to compensate. He worked on the print side of the Daily Express. Of all the hundred kind and good-natured things he said, or may have said, these are the only words of his I remember exactly. He tousled my hair, bid me stop the fleas from biting and clumped downstairs, one leg at a time. The childless couple stood discussing me in the hall. Auntie Elsie listened to Dick's account of what had been said and I sensed her familiar emphatic nod.

'What you don't know can't hurt you,' she muttered.

There was a great deal of what I did not know. My mother never came once to visit. I can remember my father arriving out of the blue one afternoon and taking me to a distant cinema to see an American war film, *Guadalcanal Diary*, which he barracked vociferously. Because he was in uniform, nobody liked to say much and in fact one or two other servicemen joined in. It was not the war they reprehended, but our principal ally's part in it. We came out into a moist autumn night and walked home 'for the exercise'. It took more than an hour, during which time my father gave everyone who scurried past in the blackout a cheerful hullo, as though he had lived in those parts all his life. To my astonishment, when we reached the house in Knightwood Crescent, he kissed me briefly on the cheek and walked away without a word.

'Well, where is he?' my aunt cried, peering down the street, as though he might be hiding behind a privet hedge.

'He's gone home,' I muttered.

She put her arms round me and crushed me for a moment and then pushed me inside.

In that walk home from the cinema was the essence of the man. In time of war, his part was that of the bluff and trustworthy constable of virtue. The uniform helped. Bulked out by an RAF greatcoat and with his shoes ringing on the pavement, he was offering passers-by a reassurance they may even have needed. Secretive by nature ('What you don't know can't hurt you'), he had risen to become a bomber navigator and a bit of a hero to his crew. But all that was, as he would have put it, his business. I did not know until many years later that when he joined the RAF he was sent to South Africa to train for aircrew. When he took me to see *Guadalcanal Diary* that afternoon, he had only just returned. Other fathers may have made an adventure out of such a long and dangerous sea trip. He never mentioned it.

In 1955, I was walking with him in Cheapside when a broken figure of a man gave a cry of recognition and tapped him for a pound, anything he could spare. He pushed the poor devil away with the flat of his hand. It was, he explained, his rear-gunner from the war years.

'Don't you want to talk to him?'

'Why should I want to do that?'

My aunt was not much more demonstrative than my father but there was a constancy in her that was enormously reassuring. She taught me multiplication and long division, always with a faint air of vexation, but I knew this to be from an inability even to imagine innumeracy. As a young woman she had crossed the river from one of the worst slums in Lambeth to work in City shops as a sales assistant. She was the model of the winsome assistant who gives a momentary lift to the customer's heart. Her mental arithmetic was dizzying and she could parcel things exquisitely. Once a month she sent her sister stiffly conventional letters outlining my situation – a cold, a new pair of shoes, failure to learn even the basics of the piano. These were written in a round and regular hand on pale blue notepaper. The letters went unanswered.

Elsie had made the transition to a respectable way of life far more successfully than my mother. In New Malden, everybody wanted to be like everybody else and set themselves the task of keeping up appearances. People nowadays speak about the sort of community this creates as stifling: I found it very comforting. When people came to tea – and they were mainly elderly ladies looking for solace from this neat and comely young woman – the sponge cake was laid out on a fretted silver stand and there were marigolds in a pot on the tea trolley. Conversation avoided anything in the least controversial and there was great nicety in knowing when to leave.

'Well, dear,' a spindly old crone said, pulling on her gloves and nodding in my direction, 'that little fellow is much happier *here*, I am quite sure.'

My father had brothers, my mother sisters. One of these worked as a riveter at Shorts and I went to stay with her for a couple of days. She took me to the works' canteen, amid great ribaldry. She was a thickset woman with hennaed hair and a wide letter-box smile.

'Your mother's a bleeding princess,' she commented, passing me her pint to sip at.

'And you can keep your opinions to yourself,' Elsie snapped when I was returned home.

'It's the war effort,' Auntie Ivy yelled, laughing uproariously. She was wearing black serge trousers and a pink sweater and chain-smoked what she called Woodies. Every knuckle on her hands had weeping scars and her nails were torn ragged to the quick.

'I hope you've been keeping your yap shut,' my aunt said, pointing a bread-knife in Ivy's face. 'And where's his tie? I sent him to you with a tie.'

I hid my face. Ivy had worn the tie with a white shirt and those same serge trousers to walk out with me and a more elderly woman called Dot. While I threw bread to the ducks, she and Dot kissed companionably and lit cigarettes from each other's stubs.

A third and far more acceptable aunt arrived one night with a Canadian naval officer and a recording of the Inkspots' latest. When it came to the line about the green grass being buried under the snow, the Canadian mimed hearty digging, sending us into fits of laughter. Then he and Dick went into the front room to talk about the war and Elsie and her sister retreated to the kitchen for what they called a conflab. My mother's name and Ivy's were several times mentioned.

The school I went to seems in retrospect suspiciously small and woebegone. Why it was housed in church premises was another enigma, for the first time I walked into a church from choice was to attend my wedding. We were not a churchy family. I assume that I was christened but I had no idea of the rites or ceremonies otherwise. (Church, as my mother pointed out in later years, was not for the likes of us. She was, by her own lights, being perfectly serious.)

One of the lessons I remember best was practising copperplate script. The examples came in a landscape format exercise book with a brown cover. The text – short sentences of useful facts – was printed above a dotted line on which we copied it with a spluttering steel nib. One example began: *Gum arabic is.* . . but whatever it is, I have completely forgotten. It was lulling and not at all unpleasant work that I associated with mists and castles. The illusion of practising some ancient art was reinforced at the centrefold of the book, where the staples were red with rust. So weak were they that a thumbnail could erase what had once been bright metal. I worried about this. The rust, the mouse-grey paper, were signs that we had been specially entrusted to keep a wavering flame alive.

The pleasure of the day was drawing landscapes with a blunt pencil, so dense with marks, so emphatic that I felt I could go and live in these pictures, walk down the winding path to some chocolate-box cottage and sit inside staring at the bombers flying overhead. They bore swastikas on their wings and tailplane. Fat bombs dropped from their bellies. In other parts of the same picture, rooks flew unconcernedly towards cauliflower trees and animals intended to be squirrels sat complacently chewing.

Phyllis drew princesses with heart-shaped bodices and empty expressions, their toes peeping out from long flounced dresses. They had speech bubbles coming from their lips saying things like *Hello!* and *I love you!* Sometimes emaciated-looking horses stood nearby. In the lunch break, which we called the dinner break, we would all go down to the basement lavatories, where Phyllis stood aghast as the more impudent girls egged on the boys to show their willies. The old dears that taught us sat upstairs, munching on chalky sandwiches and gossiping about butchers and greengrocers.

The general mood was comfy. Many afternoons passed when I felt my head rock and my eyes roll round in my skull, asleep at my desk. When this happened, Phyllis would prod me with her pencil and then look away, frowning. She had a prewar geometry set in a black leather case and would sometimes twiddle the compasses, or measure angles she had scribbled with the protractor. It passed the time. We were at war – nobody could be in any doubt about that – but floating in a bubble just a little off the ground.

'Eat that cabbage,' Elsie would order. 'There are sailors who lost their lives so's you don't have to go hungry.'

'It's from Uncle Dick's garden,' I objected.

'In general. I'm saying, in general.'

With Elsie I went to Hampton Court and – maybe it was the invasion summer – to an outdoor variety show at Motspur Park, in which a plump contortionist sank down on to the muddy boards in the splits position. When she rose, the insides of her thighs were decorated with dark smudges. Her silver knickers, the soles of her feet and the palms of her hands were likewise blackened. As she bent and writhed, a man, possibly her father, played a piano accordion accompaniment, looking ashamed and uneasy.

'Well,' Elsie commented grimly, 'she's got guts, I'll give her that.'

'She's clever, isn't she, Auntie?'

'She is if you like that sort of thing.'

One of the peculiarities of my aunt's house was that the Anderson shelter was erected indoors, filling a room that may have been originally designed as a study. In it, there were four bunks, candles, bottles of tap water and a first-aid kit in a pink biscuit tin. It was also where the Bible was kept. Once in a while Dick would open up the shelter to air it. We lived beside no marshalling yards or munitions factories but at night the Thames gleamed silver only a few miles away. Even so, the bombers gave us a miss, all but the most nervous or perhaps the most callous of them. My aunt, whose sense of the appropriate was as finely tuned as any duchess, ignored the loom of light that bespoke raids on London and would never comment on the conduct of the war. We persisted tearfully with sums and piano practice.

'Your mother can play,' she wailed once. 'What's up with you, that you can't?'

'We didn't have a piano.'

'There's a lot you don't know of what you did and didn't have. You're too dreamy by half. The world's got enough dreamboats,' she added.

Hitler, whom every child could sketch, who lived a long way away and whose every purpose was malign, eventually sent Knightwood Crescent his greetings. Dick had actually seen a V-1 rocket cut out and dive to earth over London and from that time on we slept every night in the shelter. I was put to bed on the top bunk and these two childless people sat fully dressed with their knees touching, silent and reprehending. An ack-ack battery had been posted to a playing field a few hundred yards away and would open up, firing at the exhaust flames of what everyone called flying bombs. One they missed dived over this neat and regular landscape, with its cherry trees and long lines of privet, and landed forty yards away.

'We're goners,' Elsie said in a matter-of-fact voice while the frame of the Anderson shelter still resonated.

'Rubbish,' Dick muttered. 'Open that thermos and let's have a cup of tea.'

'The gas!' she shouted suddenly.

Dick lifted me down from the bunk. We were all dusted white. He smoothed under my eyes with his thumb. Elsie struggled with the door of the shelter. It would not budge.

'Well,' she said, 'a nice thing, I must say.'

The emergency services dug us out towards mid-morning. The house had been cut in half as if by a bread-knife. The kitchen, the back room and the bedrooms above had simply disappeared, leaving a view of the tennis courts and, beyond that, the bypass. A fireman carried me into the front room, which was ankle-deep in rubble. The piano had been lifted off the floor and was pinned to the wall by long swords of glass, its whole weight supported by them.

'Bugger me,' the fireman said admiringly. He reached with his hatchet and touched just one shard and the piano fell forward with an almighty crash. Elsie and Dick stood with their arms round each other, staring out at the unaccustomed view from the foot of the missing stairs. Everything they owned had been carried away by the blast. Clothes and bed-linen decorated the branches of distant trees.

The front door was still intact and the firemen, who had climbed through the ground-floor windows to release us, obligingly kicked away the rubble so that we could open it. Where once had stood the house that belonged to the bed-ridden mother of the Radio Doctor, our sole attachment to the world of the famous, was now a huge hole in the ground. The street was ankle-deep in roof tiles.

'How many others copped it?' Dick asked.

A fireman jerked his chin at me by way of reproof and lit a dazzling white cigarette. He ruffled my hair.

'What you nice people need is a good strong cup of the old rosie. Right down there. It's all free. They're all ready for you.'

Sitting in front of the tea van, his legs tucked under a folding card table, was an ancient civilian in a white tin helmet. In front of him was a pile of useful paper and – a surreal touch – a bottle of ink should his fountain pen run dry. Hardly able to hold up his head under the weight of the tin hat, he stared at us through cruel wire glasses as we staggered up to report to the council the disappearance of half the house.

'Good morning,' he said politely.

LETTER TO PATIENCE

by **John Haynes**

seren

LETTER TO PATIENCE

by **John Haynes**

Set in Patience' Parlour, a small mud-walled bar in Northern Nigeria, at a time of political unrest, Letter to Patience is a vividly atmospheric book-length poem divided into cantos. The letter writer is in Britain, where he has returned with his Nigerian wife and children to nurse his dying father. The poem is not only a biography, or an essay on post-colonialism; it is an epic portrayal of a beautiful and troubled country and of the poet's search for meaning in difficult times.

John Haynes spent 1970 to 1988 as a lecturer in English at Ahmadu Bello University in Nigeria where he founded the literary journal Saiwa. Now back in the UK, he has continued teaching, writing and publishing and is the author of a number of books: on teaching, on style and language theory, on African poetry, stories for African children, as well as two other volumes of verse. He has won prizes in the Arvon and National Poetry Competitions.

"John Haynes' Letter to Patience was the judges' unanimous choice and a clear winner; a unique long poem of outstanding quality, condensing a lifetime of reflection and experience into a work of transporting momentum, imaginative lucidity, and consummate formal accomplishment."

Judges
Elaine Feinstein – Poet and Author
Jeremy Noel-Tod – Critic and Editor
Deryn Rees-Jones – Writer

LETTER TO PATIENCE

PREFACE

Patience' Parlour is a small mud-walled bar in Northern Nigeria in the village of Samaru. Samaru's geometrical grid of dirt streets, originally laid by the British, provides a market, a mosque, churches, beer parlours and houses for junior staff at Ahmadu Bello University across the main road. Beyond and around it is farmland where guinea corn, maize and groundnuts are grown, and you see white humped-backed cattle watched and mouth-clicked at by a ten year old boy with a stick and a raffia hat.

At the time the poem is set, Patience herself is thirtyish and has lived in Samaru for some fifteen years, first as a student, then as a lecturer in Politics at the university, a job which she has given up partly because of junta pressures on radical academics and journalists, and partly on principle: it seems to her that political education has to happen elsewhere.

Though her origins are far south in Benin City, she has got used to Samaru and it has become home, despite the periodically whipped up local prejudice against non-Hausas and non-Muslims. The bar was attacked by the so-called *Ayatollahs* in 1988, her fridge and tables wrecked, her bottles smashed in the streets, and it would have been torched had it not backed onto the property of her well-to-do Hausa landlord.

If you leave the university by the back gates, cross the road to the trestle table stalls on the other side, go alongside the market, pass the mosque, and then follow the dirt streets with their mud houses, cinemas, food hotels, stalls of kebab griddles, you get to her bar with its coloured bulbs on a board outside. It is adapted from a traditional compound with a large patio around which are set other rooms, built as separate structures. The largest, which you come into from the street entrance, forms the inside bar, essential during rainy season.

Other rooms are used for a kitchen, store room with two fridges full of bottled lager, and there is a traditional shower/toilet into which, at night, you take your candle and smear/stick it on the wall. There is electricity, but not throughout, and the main lighting comes from hurricane lamps which don't go out in the frequent power cuts. The patio is filled with rough plank tables, benches and chairs. There is a well at one end, and further rooms where Patience's teenage daughters live.

In the 1980s *Patience' Parlour* was a watering hole for radicals from the university. But the drinkers, who form the 'cast' of the poem, come from all walks of life.

The letter is set in 1993 at a time of unrest just before President Babangina was to annul the apparently perfectly fair elections which were won by Mashood Abiola who, although very far from being a man of the people, was both a Muslim and a Southerner, and so promised to be a truly national choice. Hence the unity of the nation was felt to be threatened and ethnic differences came to the fore.

The Letter Writer writes from England to which he has returned with his Nigerian wife and children to nurse his dying father. His parents had been musicians in music hall, pantomime and summer shows, his maternal grandfather a Cornish tin mining engineer who, after the collapse of the industry in 1860, went to the gold mines of South Africa, where the Letter Writer's mother was born.

The poem as a whole represents the hours from about 1 a.m. when the Letter Writer starts writing, to first light when he leaves off.

When we say "Time" we mean ourselves.
Most abstractions are simply our pseudonyms.
It is superfluous to say "Time is scytheless and
toothless." We know it. We are time.

— C P Cavafi

For nimble thought can jump both sea and land
As soon as think the place where he would be.
But, ah! thought kills me that I am not thought
— William Shakespeare, Sonnet XLIV

...the word 'I' does not have a central place in
grammar, but is a word like any other.

— Ludwig Wittgenstein

LETTER TO PATIENCE

I

The Cottage, 70 Padnell Road, Cowplain,
Hants, England, 5th May, 1993.
Patience – as I begin this yet again

now everyone's asleep, the BBC
World Service News is on its perfect line
along that line once ruled invisibly

across the globe to where that watch of mine
ticks on the inside of your wrist. Mosquito-
thin red second hand, you can refine

us to a single *now* jerk *now,* zero
meridian, across this black glass sky
with its own grid of panes and stars, and slow

pulse winking, like some tropical firefly
inching away. It could be taking this
tomorrow where time's real rules still apply:

sea, desert, savannah, airport, post office
with its dates and stamps, and then the bare
tyres bumping over dust with this homesickness

or something like it, turning *here* to *there,*
and *now* to *then,* except that now, before
even the words I'm even half aware

I want to mean form in my mouth, as sure
and speechless as the ink itself, I hear
you hearing them, as if I'm some folk-lore

style ghost that needs no corridor to steer
through space or time, as if the see-through head
reflected like a kite on this sky near

us both, might bring these words not yet quite said.
My ghost, the paper soul of me that slips
away, leaving its cell of bone for dead

awhile, here, two o'clock, the first few pips
before the news again on BBC,
and hands typing by touch. No, fingertips.

II

Go little spirit, then, and I can see
the candles wobbling on those stalls outside
the campus gate, the piles of *Ambi, Maggi*

Cubes, tea bags, the mosquito coils, the dried
crayfish in twists of polythene, the tray
with Saddam Hussein's face on it, the fried

yam clicking in its oil as Mamma Ture
bends village style down to her wide black pans,
her toes spread out, her bum hoisted, her grey

logs nothing now but beards, the Peak Milk cans
with tugging wicks of cotton wool, the flare
of charcoal from the suya sellers' fans,

house-fronts swaying in fumes, through pepper air
the coloured lightbulbs rattling on your bar
making the tree in front as vague as hair,

the drain wrinkly with rainbows, the car
sunk to its rusted wheel hubs in the dust,
door jamb, handbills for *Double Crown* and *Star*,

thin slits of light, reggae, voices, a gust
of laughter. As if I could make that bit
of threadbare cloth push back, as if I just

might feel the wall resist my palm, its grit
just shifting first, then underneath, the glow
of that sun right down in the mud of it....

III

As if it's all there still, a road, a row
of houses with the horns and plasticine-
like joins of walls, as if the radio

is wrong, or here has not been touched, there's been
no rioting, no churches have been torched,
no beer tipped in the gutters, no *shebeen*

(as they called it) left with its roofbeams scorched
and smoking among broken chairs and glass,
no *women from Hollywood Clob* debauched

and stoned for harlots, as if men with scars
and home made bandages had not crammed Kano
junction struggling into buses, cars

taxies, mammy wagons. I don't know
where to address this to you in Benin
City, Patience. I'll send it care of Joe

at the department, if in fact Joe's in
the office still – yes, I know, for some clerk
to crumple up and lob towards the bin

with all the others which have this postmark
and nothing in them but the words? And yet,
it's just words, isn't it – the helpless stark

unlikelihood that they will ever get
to you – that makes me weigh the empty air
and shape of each. As if to hedge a bet.

IV

My daughter's new Bob Marley hair
beads click each time she moves her head, asleep
against the broad arm of the easy chair.

This was their Music Room and we still keep
the Francis Day & Hunter songs in place
along the shelves. My childhood tunes are deep

into the walls and floorboards here, their base
between pantos and summer shows. They look
from sterling silver frames into the space

from which applause should come. Outside, a hook
and chain suspends *The Cottage* in the ye
old letters of a children's story book.

Sometimes we act them out at bedtime, Ratty,
Badger, Mole, hallooing *Hey you fellows*
from the garden in their good chap RP,

those upright beasts dressed in Victorian clothes
that make you laugh. Lara's got a green
felt Mr Toad. His humbug eyes don't close

for all she hugs, just blink back as this screen
blinks, towards shelves of *Tarzan*, paper music,
Porter, Gershwin, Berlin, Kern – Dad's has-been

ancestors whose *Darkies* clinked an Afrik
banjo gut as if their fingering
might just retune the sun's own rays to pick

out human intervals along a string
and fret, just like the ancient profs, with skin
almost as dark, who made the numbers sing

for young Pythagoras when he sat in
their bars – like yours – drunk to the selfless essence
floating from his body like a djin

in timeless *now*. Exactly now, Patience,
I too want to make all Africa narrow
to a mud walled bar. There's arrogance.

V

As I think the thought of it a shadow
tumbler prints the creosoted top
of a plank table with those little hollow

ovals like a spider's web. A drop
of fat bursts into charcoal smoke that lifts
in rags across the voices, reggae, pop

of bottle tops, recalling, as it drifts
and thins away, some textbook entropy
stopped in the photograph's siftings and shifts

here, far off, at a screen, in memory
where there's no time, only a sense of sight
that's always there behind the eyes exactly

now, your stiff headtie, your nyash wrapped tight
in *george* as always, the wet bottles gleam-
ing in your elbows, now as every night

both there and here, both real and in the dream
in which your ghost is standing there again
unknown to you, as in a spotlight beam,

caught in the slime and wrinkles of a brain
that isn't yours, and synapse pulse and node
dissolve you Star Trek style into a rain

then in its other time and space reload
each cliché over cliché, till it's you,
again, half juju and half genome code,

now moving through the bar with *esewu*
in little wooden tubs. The gobbets shine
and steam and wobble in the soup, grey-blue

goat lip, goat nostril, goat eye, ear. "Fine-fine
na you go mek book, John, wid dis kain brain
for dey insai." And yet it isn't mine,

is it, nor yours, this picture from a chain
of nerves that spreads and spreads out of my head
like pins and needles, that I can't contain?

VI

"The bar is what you're going to miss," you said,
"not me," but that's wrong isn't it, to draw
lines around people (even if they're dead),

as if I'd miss the place you live in more
than you, when there's no line between at all
and that's something that *you* kept saying, *your*

philosophy, the sense of floor, mud wall,
dust road as who we are, the kites' long cry
at harmattan, the beggar's rhythmic call

outside Alhaji Kowa's store, this *I*
that floats and enters you from just as far
as ever, dear one, shapeless as the sigh

that lifts out of your mouth, out of the bar,
out of the rusted corrugated zinc
and mixes with some wailing armoured car

out on the road, and then the first tink-tink
of birds, the cockerel's call, none of it you,
except that when I think of it I think

it is and not the old *femme noir, femme nue*
'Afrique', no, something shared in spite of skin
colour, and Lugard's maxim gun, or *through*

just those, is it? I think so, what we're in,
as what we are. And so I'm writing this
Magana Jari Ce, am I, to spin

you into words? A spell, a selfishness
to try and keep you there, or rather here,
closing my eyes with lust to see, miss

you, sharper – no, the bar, music, the beer?
Or it's an elegy for someone dead
for all I know, for all I fear to fear.

NOTES

Canto I
a single now: Nigeria and Britain fall along the same longitude
and, during British summer time, have the same clock time.
Canto IV
Pythagoras: Pythagoras is thought to have visited and brought
mathematical ideas from Arabia and possibly further east.
Canto V
nyash: Pidgin: bum
esewu: Calabar dish made with chopped goat head and spiced
sauce.
Fine-fine na… Pidgin. You'll make books very well, John, with
this kind of brain inside you.

ACKNOWLEDGEMENTS

Acknowledgements are due to the editors of the following
publications in which parts of this poem, some of them reshaped
since, have been published: *Ambit, Critical Quarterly, London
Magazine, Poetry Review, Poetry Wales, Stand Magazine, Wasafiri,
Tying the Song* (Enitharmon, 2000).

Thanks are due also to John Greening, Matthew Sweeney, Thomas
Lynch, and Mimi Khalvati for criticism.

SET IN STONE

by **Linda Newbery**

David Fickling Books

SET IN STONE

by **Linda Newbery**

When naïve and impressionable artist Samuel Godwin accepts the position of tutor to the daughters of wealthy Ernest Farrow, he does not suspect that he's walking into a web of deception. He is drawn to the lives of the three young women who live at Fourwinds: Charlotte Agnew, the governess; demure Juliana, the elder daughter; and younger sister, Marianne, passionate, wilful and erratic. Yet it's not only the people who entrance Samuel. The house, Fourwinds, is an inspiring piece of architecture that looms large in the lives of those who encounter it. It is not long before Samuel and Charlotte uncover secrets that are both horrifying and dangerous to all...

Linda Newbery was born in 1952 and brought up in Epping, Essex. The author of more than twenty books for children and young adults, Linda also reviews fiction for the Times Educational Supplement and other publications, and tutors courses for writers of all ages. Linda lives with her husband and three cats in rural Northamptonshire.

"As beautifully crafted as one of the statues adorning the house in the story, this emotionally charged narrative will thrill all lovers of intelligent fiction."

Judges
Geraldine Brennan – Books Editor, TES
Adèle Geras – Novelist and Children's Writer
Brian Pattinson – Proprietor, The Book House (Thame)
Nancy Netherwood (Young Judge) – CBBC Newsround, 'Presspacker'
Nathan Sutton (Young Judge) – CBBC Newsround, 'Presspacker'

> *'To handle stone is to handle the stuff of life and death,*
> *of time and change, the mysteries of the Earth itself...'*

Prologue

The Wild Girl
1920

Samuel Godwin
Watercolours and Oil Paintings
Private View

The poster is almost obscured by the press of people entering the gallery. Wineglass in hand, I position myself to one side, a spectator at my own exhibition; as the guests file in, I assume a genial smile, and prepare to wear it for the duration of the evening.

Nowadays there are many such occasions, enough to make me droop at the prospect of yet another. How easily we tire of novelties, once their gloss has faded! Twenty years ago, I dreamed of this tedious social duty as the height of my aspiration. If I had thought then, at the start of my career, that people would flock to see my work – and not only to look, but to pay handsomely for it; that I should be fêted, flattered, invited to dine, to comment, to make speeches; that I should be regarded as someone touched by the Muse, not quite in the run of common men – I should have thought it a wishful dream. But this has become the pattern of my life, no longer yearned for. My name, now, seems to stand apart from me. It is a valued signature, two words that command a price; its syllables are spoken by people who consider themselves connoisseurs.

'Ah, Mr Godwin!' The woman bearing down on me, social smile stretching her lipsticked mouth, scarf draped artfully around her neck and secured with a brooch, is of the wearisome type I often meet at such viewings. 'Let me have your attention, before you're quite besieged! I am so curious – do tell me . . .' Manicured fingers touch my sleeve; perfume mingles with cigarette smoke. 'The Wild Girl. She intrigues me so very much. Who is she, I wonder? Do tell.'

I avert my eyes from the archness of her gaze, and block my ears to her gush. Across the gallery, my Wild Girl stares at me from her ebony frame. Although her expression is seared into my mind, although my own hand made every brushstroke that defines her, I cannot look on her without feeling a fresh twist of pain. Her hair, of that rich, extraordinary shade I used to amuse myself by defining – the colour of newly opened chestnuts in their cases, of beech leaves against snow, of polished pennies, of a kestrel's wing – tumbles over her shoulders. Her eyes, not quite green, not quite blue, hold mine in a blend of exultation and pleading. This is my reason for painting her: to hold this moment in suspension, to keep for ever the possibilities it holds.

In the next instant it will be too late. Her plea will remain unanswered, and I will have failed.

My heart clenches.

I do this to her, my Wild Girl. I bring her to these fashionable galleries, I expose her to these scavengers with their ravenous eyes and their predatory cheque-books. Do they really see her? Twenty years ago she would have been as invisible as the rest of my work. Now, because she carries my name (but not her own), she is the object of speculation. Fickle fashion has decreed that my work is collectable. *The Wild Girl* is a desirable commodity.

But not for sale. No, never.

'Come, now, Mr Godwin!' My inquisitor plucks at my sleeve and peers closely into my face. 'Please don't be coy! Is there a story here, I wonder? Such a beauty – she is someone you loved, maybe? She is a real girl – yes, surely.'

I catch the eye of the gallery owner. Knowing how I dislike being cornered, he threads his way towards us, summoning a waiter to refill our glasses. I see my chance to escape.

'She is herself,' I answer, sidling away. 'She is someone I met many years ago.'

Set in Stone

Chapter One

Fourwinds
June, 1898

(Samuel Godwin)

It was an impulse stirred by the moon over the Downs that made me decide to complete my journey on foot. Such a night as this, I thought, standing outside the railway station in the moonlight that seemed almost liquid silver, is too great a gift to ignore behind drawn curtains and closed doors. It is to be fully experienced with all senses – lived, inhaled, absorbed.

It had been arranged that my new employer, Mr Farrow, would send a pony-chaise to meet me, but a series of misfortunes had delayed my arrival. My London train had departed late, and I had missed my connection; he must have given up expecting me until the morrow. At this hour there was no conveyance of any kind to be seen. At first wondering whether to spend the night in the local tavern and continue next morning, I then had the idea of walking. I asked the stationmaster to put my trunk aside until morning, explained that my destination was Fourwinds, and showed him the address.

'Mile or so up the lane there, all uphill, then turn left down a rough old track by a copse. Stick on that track and it'll bring you to the gates.' He seemed to feel unduly put upon by my request to store the trunk, and began, with a grudging air, to haul it towards the ticket office.

'I shall send for it in the morning,' I told him.

He accepted without comment the coin I gave him for his trouble. I shouldered the small pack in which I had my necessaries, and set off at once, past a coaching inn – with no coaches to be seen – and out of Staverton in the direction he had indicated.

As the sounds from the inn and the lights from the stationmaster's house receded, I found myself alone, and very tiny, beneath the vast, starred expanse of sky. Coming from the London suburb of Sydenham, where I had lived all my life, I had rarely experienced such isolation as this, such silence. And yet, as my ears attuned to my new surroundings, it was not silence I heard: my feet trod steadily on the stony road; I heard the hooting of an owl, the screech of some unseen creature in the verge, the faintest rustle of grasses sighing against each other. I was on a high, open road, curving over the swell of hillside that I saw as the flanks of some prehistoric animal, deep in slumber. The moonlight was so strong as to throw my shadow beside me on the road as a mute companion; and so I found myself not quite alone after all, taking a childish pleasure in my shadow-self as it matched me stride for stride. I could see quite clearly my road curving ahead, and the clump of trees, inky black, that marked my turning point.

From here, my track took me sharply left. Chalky and bare, it formed rough undulations over the ground, leading me to the brow of a low hill; chalk stones grated underfoot. Fourwinds, the house at which I was to take up employment, apparently lay in a very isolated spot, for I could see no sign of habitation, no friendly lamp in a farmhouse window, no plume of smoke from a shepherd's humble croft. I felt very conscious of travelling from one stage of my life to the next: every step away from the road carried me farther from London, my mother and sister, the art school and my friends there; each tread brought me nearer to the house and its inhabitants, of which, and of whom, I knew very little.

Reaching the highest point of the track, I glanced about me; and saw now that my track descended into woodland, dense and dark. The stationmaster had mentioned no wood; but perhaps the omission could be ascribed to his hurry to finish work for the night. I hesitated; then, as sure as I could be that I had made no mistake, continued on my path down into the valley and the shadows of the trees.

Darkness swallowed me; the branches arched high overhead; I saw only glimpses of the paler sky through their tracery. My feet crunched beech mast. I smelled the coolness of mossy earth, and heard the trickle of water close by. As my eyes accustomed themselves to dimmer light, I saw that here, on the lower ground, a faint mist hung in the air, trapped perhaps beneath the trees. I must be careful not to stray from the path, which I could only dimly discern; but before many minutes had passed, wrought-iron gates reared ahead of me, set in a wall of flint. Though I had reached the edge of the wood, my way was barred. The gate must, however, be unlocked, as my arrival was expected.

I peered through the scrollwork of the gates. The track, pale and broad, wound between specimen trees and smooth lawns; I had some distance still to walk, it seemed. The mist clung to the ground, and the trees seemed rooted in a vaporous swamp. I tried the fastening; the left-hand gate swung open with a loud, grating squeal that echoed into the night.

At the same moment another sound arose, competing for shrillness with the gate's protest: a sound to make my heart pound and my nerves stretch taut. It was a wailing shriek that filled my head and thrummed in my ears; close enough to make me shrink against the gate, which I pushed open to its fullest extent against the shadows of the wall. Whether the cry was animal or human, I could not tell. If human, it was a sound of terrible distress, of unbearable grief. I felt the hairs prickle on the back of my neck, my eyes trying to stare in all directions at once. Instinct told me to hunch low till the danger passed. Dropped into such strangeness, I had acquired, it seemed, the impulse of a wild creature to hide myself and survive whatever perils were near. The metal bit into my hands as I clung to the gate. Attempting to retain a clear head, I reminded myself that I was unfamiliar with the sounds of the countryside at night. It must be a fox, a badger, some creature yowling in hunger or pain.

The next instant, all my senses quickened again as I discerned a movement in the shadow: a movement that resolved itself into a cloaked figure – slender, female – rushing towards me. As I had not seen her approach, she must have been lurking by the wall. In the confusion of the moment, the thought flitted across my mind that this might be a ghostly presence – the setting, the eerie light, the ground-veiling mist that made her seem to advance without feet, all contributed to this fancy. Since she appeared intent on collision, I reached out both hands to ward her off; but, unswerving, she grabbed me by one arm. I saw that she was not woman but girl – an adolescent girl, with hair wild and loose under her hooded cloak – and no ghost, but a living person, breathing, panting, alarmed. For it must have been she who had shrieked.

'Help – please help me!' she begged, tightening her grip on my arm, and peering close into my face.

At once a different instinct was aroused – for now I must be protector, not prey. 'Madam, I am at your service,' I assured her, looking around, steeling myself to confront possible attackers.

'Where is it?' she implored me, her eyes searching mine. 'Where?'

'Madam – miss! Please explain what is distressing you, and I shall gladly give what help I can.'

Thinking that I might take her with me to Fourwinds, where assistance could be summoned, I tried to free myself from her grasp in order to close the gate behind me, but she seemed equally determined that it should stay open. For a few moments we struggled; I was surprised by her strength and tenacity. I tried to shake her off; I almost flung her from me; but she was like a terrier set on a fox, and would not be detached.

'Have you seen him?' she pleaded.

'If you might stand back and allow me to -' I began, but she burst out with, 'No! No! I cannot stop searching, while he is roaming free -'

'Who?' I enquired, looking about me again.

'The West Wind!' she replied, in a tone of impatience; and she tilted her head and gazed about in anguish, as if expecting a gusting presence to manifest itself above our heads.

'I beg your pardon?'

'The West Wind!' she repeated. 'He must be found – captured, and secured!'

The poor young lady must be deranged, I realized, suffering from fits or delusions – had escaped, maybe, from some institution. For why else should a young woman of her tender years be out alone at night, so far from habitation, and on such an extraordinary mission?

With the gate closed at last, I thought it best to humour her. 'I'm afraid I have no idea where to look,' I answered.

She turned her head rapidly this way and that; she gazed at me again. 'Who are you?' she demanded, almost rudely.

'My name is Samuel Godwin, and I am on my way to Fourwinds. A Mr Ernest Farrow lives there.'

'Oh! To Fourwinds!' she repeated, as one struck by an amazing coincidence – although we were, presumably, in the grounds of that very house. For a few moments she stared at me; then, abruptly, her manner changed. She stepped back, making an effort to breathe more calmly; she straightened herself and seemed to grow taller; she became, in effect, a different person. 'Then – you are my new tutor.' She extended a hand to shake mine, as formally as if we were being introduced in a drawing room. 'I am very pleased indeed to meet you – I am Marianne Farrow, one of your two pupils. Let me lead you to the house, and introduce you to my father and sister.'

Chapter Two

A Disturbance

(Charlotte Agnew)

Devoted to Mr Farrow though I was, I could not deny that he had some rather exasperating habits. Chief among these was his failure to communicate matters of pressing interest to others in the house. It was typical of him that he did not think to mention that an art tutor from London would be joining us at Fourwinds until two days before the young man's arrival.

My employer summoned me to his office, then, as was his wont, carried on writing, bent over his desk, without so much as glancing up at me. Used to his manner, I waited patiently. The delay allowed me to study the details of his appearance: his meticulous attire, his close-curling dark hair, his frown of concentration, and the strong fingers that gripped the pen. The bold, angular script that issued from the pen-nib was a part of his character.

After a few moments he looked up. 'Ah, yes,' he said, bestowing on me the briefest of glances; at once his attention was back with the papers on his desk, which he began to tidy into folders and drawers. 'There is to be an addition to our household, Charlotte! A bedroom must be prepared, and all made ready. A Mr Samuel Godwin will be taking up residence here, to instruct Juliana in drawing and painting, and to carry out some commissions I have in mind. He is a young artist, trained at the Slade School of Art – I have the highest expectations of him. He will be with us on Monday afternoon. Please tell Mrs Reynolds to make arrangements.'

Clearly, no further information was forthcoming; he expected me to have no opinion on the matter. Giving me a nod and a smile, he picked up a letter, tutted with impatience at what he read there, then, when I gave a modest cough to attract his attention, seemed surprised to find that I was still in the room; his eyebrows rose quizzically.

'For how long,' I enquired, 'will this Mr Godwin be staying?'

'Oh, I have engaged him for an indefinite period,' he replied. 'The art lessons will take place daily. Juliana needs taking out of herself, and we will all appreciate a change of company.'

'Marianne loves to draw and paint,' I reminded him.

'Yes, of course,' he replied. 'Well, she can take part in the lessons too.'

'Are the young ladies aware that Mr Godwin is expected?'

'No, I haven't yet mentioned it,' said he, taking an envelope out of the bureau drawer, and writing an address with rapid slashes of his pen. 'I shall tell them at dinner. If you prefer to tell them sooner, please do.'

Dismissed, I closed the door behind me, and stood for a moment on the half-landing before going down to the morning room. If I confess that my first reaction was of displeasure, this may seem surprising; our life at Fourwinds was uneventful, with Mr Farrow often away from home, and few visitors to break our seclusion. The arrival of a young man from London might be expected to provoke interest and expectation. Certainly, when I conveyed the news to my two charges, Marianne was greatly excited. 'An artist!' she exclaimed, several times, as though our new arrival were closer akin to deity than to mortal man. 'Is he famous? Is he handsome, do you suppose? How do you picture him, Charlotte? I think he must have luxuriant dark hair, and a bold twinkling eye. What will he think of us? And he comes from London! – I fear he may find us rather dull. Are you not afraid he will, Juley?'

Juliana said little, and I even less. Mr Farrow's purpose in this arrangement was, I found, perplexing. He could without much difficulty have engaged a tutor to come to the house in the afternoons, as often as he thought beneficial; it hardly seemed necessary for the artist to come and live with us. Yet it was characteristically generous of Mr Farrow, once having thought of a scheme, to spare no expense in carrying it out. His daughters were everything to him; and, as usual, this thought provoked in me a flash of warmth, sharpened with envy. Such is my lot; these jealous pangs are the cost of my happiness here – or, if it is not complete happiness, it is the nearest to it I have ever known.

My hard-won equilibrium was likely to be upset by the intrusion of a stranger. The circumstances of my life have taught me to keep my own secrets, and to respect those of others. With few acquaintances, I value those I can trust; these number very few, and are to be found within the confines of Fourwinds. I did not look forward to admitting a newcomer to our circle.

After a period of reflection, however, it occurred to me that I might find companionship in the new arrangement. Someone in my position can be rather isolated in a household; neither a member of the family, nor one of the domestic servants, she occupies a somewhat in-between role. Mr Godwin would find himself similarly placed. I allowed myself to conjecture that he and I might walk in the gardens together, or enjoy quiet conversations in the drawing room after the girls had retired to bed.

This foolishness was most unlike me, and experience has taught me that high expectations are frequently thwarted; therefore, I prepared myself for our Mr Godwin to be disagreeable, arrogant, or weak-featured, to have an irritating laugh, or odious breath, or a pompous, self-regarding air. Thus, I was pleasantly surprised when he entered the vestibule of Fourwinds. It was late at night, so late that I had assumed he would not after all appear until the morrow. Mr Farrow had retired to his room, and I was roving the house in search of Marianne, who had slipped away while I was reading. No hooves had been heard approaching, nor the rumble of wheels, so I was startled when the front door opened to admit both Marianne and a somewhat bemused-looking young man. Marianne was flushed and excitable, and I knew at once that she had had one of her wandering fits. It was my fault; yet how could I prevent such escapes without either dogging the poor girl's heels like a shepherd's collie, or keeping her under lock and key?

'Charlotte!' she said, coming towards me eagerly. 'Here is Mr Godwin – I found him outside. Such a long walk he's had – all the way from Staverton!'

The newcomer stood, hat in hand, just inside the door. Like most visitors to Fourwinds, though there are not many, he was gazing about him in some surprise at the height and space of the entrance hall, having expected, I suppose, a traditional country mansion, which this most assuredly is not.

'Good evening, Mr Godwin,' I said, extending my hand. 'Welcome to Fourwinds. My name is Charlotte Agnew – I am companion to the Misses Farrow, and Marianne's governess. What regrettable inconvenience you have suffered by having to walk! You must be very tired.'

We shook hands while I made this speech. His hand was warm, his grip firm. He was a tall young man, well-built but not stocky, with springy hair, rich brown in colour, brushed back from a shapely forehead. His eyes were grey, his nose straight and his mouth determined; when he answered, his voice was deep and well modulated.

'I am very glad to meet you, Miss Agnew,' said he. 'No, I am not tired in the least. I preferred to walk on such a beautiful night. But I am sorry to disturb your household so late.'

Though certainly not the flamboyant figure Marianne had imagined, Samuel Godwin was pleasing in person and manner.

Although Juliana had yet to set eyes on him, I saw that he had already made a good impression on her younger sister. While I made enquiries about his baggage, summoned Mrs Reynolds to serve his supper and asked her to call Juliana from her room, Marianne watched attentively, her eyes resting with fascination on his face, then turning to mine. Yes, I thought, she is quite engrossed with him, impulsive creature that she is, after an acquaintance of some five or ten minutes.

Mr Godwin gave a detailed explanation of the circumstances that had delayed his arrival, and apologized again; I assured him that it did not matter in the least, and that we were pleased he had arrived safely. With Marianne following, I showed him to his room, which was on the second floor, on the east side of the house, with a view over the gardens and the lake. Afterwards we returned to the dining room, where Mrs Reynolds had set out a meal of cold meat, cheese and pickles. After pouring him a glass of wine, and another for myself, I sat with him at table.

'Marianne,' I said, as she seemed inclined to linger, 'your sister has not come down. Will you go and tell her Mr Godwin has arrived?'

She nodded, and left us.

'I have never seen a more beautiful house!' Mr Godwin remarked. He looked around him at the clean stone arch of the fireplace, at the bay window with its cushioned seats, and the heavy curtains that fell to the floor; he stroked a hand over the smooth-grained wood of the chair adjacent to his. 'Everything chosen with such care! Mr Farrow is a man of very decided tastes. That was evident when I met him in London.'

'Most assuredly he is,' I agreed.

'He is not at home this evening?'

'He is; but he has already retired. I'm afraid we had quite given you up until tomorrow. Please, begin,' I told him, indicating his plate.

Mr Godwin picked up his knife and fork, but stopped there.

'Miss Agnew,' he began tentatively, 'I think I ought to tell you that when I first came across Marianne – I beg your pardon, I mean the younger Miss Farrow – she seemed in great distress. I met her at some distance from the house – wandering, quite alone, and crying out in anguish. I thought at first she was being attacked, or threatened in some way -' He broke off. 'But I see that you are not surprised by this information?'

'Thank you for your kind concern, Mr Godwin,' I replied. 'It is good of you to share it with me. As you are aware, Mr Farrow has engaged you principally to teach his elder daughter, Juliana. Juliana is very different in character from her sister; you will find her quiet and amenable. Marianne, on the other hand, is somewhat excitable, as you have seen.'

'Excitable, indeed!'

'It is merely a phase – it will pass. But you need not concern yourself unduly. She has not always been thus afflicted; it seems to be a malaise of adolescence. She has an over-active imagination – that is all.'

'All, Miss Agnew? What is to be more feared than the excesses of imagination? Where can anyone be less easily helped than when lost in fear? For the mind can produce terrors to eclipse anything found in the material world. Can nothing be done to help her?'

'A doctor is in regular attendance,' I told him, rather crisply. 'She has the best possible care. Her welfare is my responsibility; yours is for her drawing and painting. Here at Fourwinds, where everyone knows her ways, she is in little danger of harming herself.'

'And yet she suffers such torment. Poor girl!' I saw sympathy flare in his grey eyes.

'It was unfortunate,' I continued, 'that you first met her in this over-stimulated state. She is otherwise an agreeable and most charming girl.'

Still he had not taken one mouthful. 'I cannot help thinking that Mr Farrow might have warned me of this, when he interviewed me in London,' he remarked, 'since Miss Farrow is to be my pupil. He gave no hint of it.'

'I suppose he did not wish to give unnecessary alarm. In the present circumstances, Marianne has become a little over-excited. It is probable that from now on she will be quite herself, and you will see only the pleasant, attentive young woman who left us just now. Come, please begin your meal.'

He began to eat; at first with polite reserve, apparently conscious of himself as the only diner; then with appreciative eagerness.

'What did you mean, Miss Agnew,' he asked me after a few mouthfuls, 'when you referred just now to the present circumstances?'

'I meant, of course, your arrival,' I told him. 'We are an isolated household here, Mr Godwin. We see few visitors. The sisters spend most of their time in each other's company, and in mine. They rarely meet men; especially, I may say, young men. Juliana, you will find, is a mature and sensible young woman, but Marianne is very different. She is an impressionable girl; her imagination is fed by stories and romances; she likes to indulge in daydreams. It would not be surprising if, thrown into the company of a personable young man, she were to behave, let us say, inappropriately. You see, I know her well. We must trust you, Mr Godwin, to keep within the bounds of propriety.'

He understood me at once. A deep blush crept over his face; he looked at me in consternation, seemed about to speak, but said nothing. Why, I thought, he is hardly more than a boy. Then something even more startling occurred; my own face, as though in sympathy with his discomfiture, began to flush hotly. Averting my gaze from his, I busied myself with wiping an imaginary smear from my wineglass. I am not given to blushing; it is my pride to be always discreet, detached, the perfect employee, almost invisible when I choose to be. At this moment I was far from invisible, with my face flaming like a beacon.

'Miss Agnew, you have my word that -' he began, but was interrupted by the opening of the door. Marianne burst in, followed by Juliana.

'Here he is, Juley!' said Marianne, almost pushing her sister towards us.

Composing myself, I carried out the introductions. Juliana, very self-conscious, very pale, looked wan and lifeless next to her sister's vivacity. She gave only the most fleeting smile as she shook Mr Godwin's hand, and enquired whether he found his room satisfactory. He, I saw, was intrigued by the contrast between the two. Juliana, as told to me by Mrs Reynolds, and confirmed by the photograph in Mr Farrow's study, resembled her mother; Marianne, with her vivid colouring and stronger features, took after her father.

Watching, I was alert to the glances criss-crossing in all directions. Marianne was looking at Mr Godwin with a complacent, almost proprietorial air; he, repeating his compliments about the house, was turning from one sister to the other; Juliana, venturing to give him only the shyest of glances, now lifted her eyes and looked at me directly, in what looked like a plea for help.

'Come, now,' I said briskly. 'It is late, and you have had a long and tiring journey, Mr Godwin. Let us retire – if you have finished your meal. We shall make each other's acquaintance more fully in the morning.'